SEO and what you should know.

By L.G. Herring

To Chris, who said I could write a book on SEO. Your support made this happen; thank you.

Contents:

Chapter	Page

SEO

Preface

SEO (or Search Engine Optimisation) is a marketing strategy websites and blogs use in order to be at the top of search engine results for certain keywords and phrases. Search engines list results based on their own criteria of relevance and understanding of the industry.

This book looks to outline the procedure in an uncomplicated manner helping to further understand the processes behind the market of Search Engine Optimisation.

It is worth noting that the procedures and steps outlined in this book were correct at the time of publishing and can be opened for interpretation. Research has been conducted in order to justify and certify certain areas of search engine optimisation yet this is not an exclusive measure.

The search engine industry is ever evolving and changing to suit the needs of supply and demand so this book should only be taken as a light illustration as different websites require different volumes of optimisation so there is no one size fits all.

The author holds no responsibility or liability for any misinterpretation of this book that may lead to the penalisation of websites from search engines based on excessive use of particular areas of search engine optimisation as outlined in the various update sections.

What is SEO?

SEO is Search Engine Optimisation. This is a process that confuses many online marketers and it is ever changing, so it is imperative to get it right and keep getting it right according to the guidelines and information search engines set out to help you rank well. This book will run through the overall premise of SEO in more detail so you can gain a firmer understanding of what it is, and how to best implement it. It's worth noting that SEO isn't an exact science and it is ever evolving, so it's worth covering the bases before trying to cover the more intricate details of this wonderful marketing strategy.

Chances are you've used search engines online to find the answer to a query you may have had, and if you have used some of the major search engines such as Google, Yahoo, Bing, or ask (to name a few) then you've already been exposed to search engine optimisation without necessarily realising it. After typing your query and hitting return (or clicking search), you're presented with a list of links to various websites relevant to the query you have made (Most commonly, people use the Google search engine, but SEO applies to all search engines across the web). Examples would look like this (please turn to the next page):

Google | Darlington Used Cars

Web   Maps   Shopping   News   Images   More ▾   Search tools

About 1,160,000 results (0.62 seconds)

KIA in **Darlington** - Kia.co.uk
www.kia.co.uk/**UsedCars** ▾
Request Your Test Drive Today! Visit KIA S G Petch in **Darlington**
Explore The New KIA Range - Find Great KIA Offers - KIA Approved Used Cars

Darlington Used Cars - autoexposure.co.uk
users.autoexposure.co.uk/ ▾
The Smart Way to Buy! The **Used Cars** Dealer You Can Trust.

Used Cars In **Darlington** - RMBAuto.co.uk
www.rmbauto.co.uk/Autoparc ▾
Visit RMB Autoparc Today For A Huge Choice Of **Used Cars** At Low Prices

Used cars for sale in **Darlington** - Autotrader
www.autotrader.co.uk › Buying › UK › North East › County Durham ▾
Used cars for sale in **Darlington**, find your perfect **used car** today from our wide range
of **second hand cars** available in **Darlington** on Auto Trader, the UK's No.1 ...

Used Cars for sale in County Durham - Gumtree
www.gumtree.com/**cars**/county-durham ▾
Find the latest **used** and new **cars** for sale in County Durham on Gumtree. See the
latest private ... yesterday. Save. Remove. Peugeot 307 1.4s **Darlington** ...

Comerford Car Sales: Used Cars **Darlington**, **Used Car** ...
www.comerford**cars**.co.uk/ ▾
Comerford Car Sales is a **used car** dealer in **Darlington** stocking a wide range of
second hand cars at great prices. Visit us today for affordable **used cars** in ...

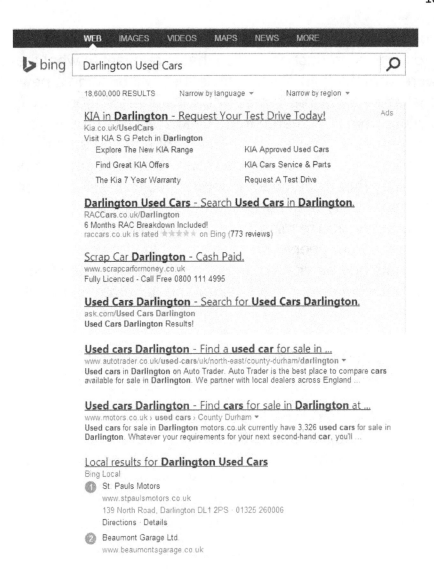

You are presented with a list of results (as seen above) and you chose the one that seems most relevant to your search.

Many people ask why SEO is important to their website and why they should even consider implementing any Search strategies. The answer is simple; as users find you through a search engine mechanic and you are providing a product or service that is relevant to what they were searching for, it's plausible they will become a new customer, and what's more you will generate more new visitors from that search term. Ultimately this means you will generate more visitors and revenue. If you aren't found through search engines then you're not going to be found by these searchers meaning you're missing out on the opportunity of generating new business. More importantly, you're missing out on generating new business from people who are searching for your products and services directly and they may instead be presented with your competitors and generate them with custom.

SEO incorporates many other online marketing strategies such as online advertising, social media marketing and online PR, but fundamentally, Search Engine Optimisation is the leading marketing strategy. Google have hundreds of factors they take into consideration when ranking the results for a particular query. Only the search engines know each and all of the factors the search engines look for, but there are many that have been released to the general public by the search engines to help you on your ranking journey. Essentially this means that there are many ways to rank effectively on the search engines and there is no definitive path you must take in order to rank well, as it is entirely subjective.

Google themselves provide many insights as to how you can rank well, and they have an inside search page that breaks SEO down into three key factors, crawling to index, algorithms and fighting spam. These will be covered in more detail throughout.

Fundamentally, the first process any search engine tries to establish is the meaning behind your search. It uses many technologies to best assess this such as knowledge graph which helps devise the purpose behind your search. You have probably already been exposed to this by the way Google pre-empts your search by providing you with a list of suggestions under what you are searching like such:

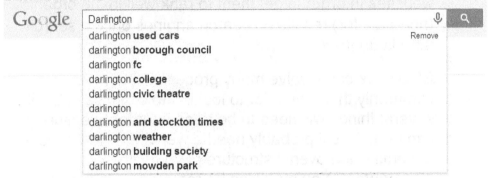

Search engines are working continuously on finding more effect ways to predict what you may be searching for in order to find you the information/results you require more accurately.

Search engines also take into consideration the device you are using to present you with the most relevant results. Desktop devices can access entire sites, and mobile devices have to access mobile versions of the sites so search engines are able to provide you with more relevant results based on the device you are using, as desktop sites don't function well on mobile devices and mobile sites don't function well on desktop devices.

Search engine optimisation essentially aims to provide work behind your site to get you within the first few results on the search engines for the searches you are hoping to put your website in front of. This work includes optimising your site through site structure and architecture, keyword research, link building, unique content, anchor text and site quality.

Fundamentally, SEO is an acronym that stands for Search Engine Optimisation. This is the process behind websites in order to get them to rank well in the organic (non-paid for) results on search engines once a search term is queried.

SEO work can involve many processes but more commonly than not, prior to looking to optimise your site, several things will need to be done in order to ensure you can rank. You'll probably need a website review covering the entire and overall structure of your site, and indeed your content. You may also be required to do keyword research and undergo SEO training in order to rank well. Keyword research is an intricate process that can seem daunting, but is very much worthwhile to succeeding online.

It's worth noting that the results displayed on Google are both organic and paid. Paid results (from PPC) will have no effect on your website's organic Search Engine Ranking Positions (SERPs). SEO from search engine's points of view is free. They rank you according to relevance, how natural your site looks and by popularity.

If you're looking on information on how to rank well, Google provide many great insights. Their Webmaster Tools, Webmaster Central blog and discussion forum have substantial amounts of information on how best to optimise your site for organic listings. Of course, you'd need to have an extensive understanding of the search marketing industry in order to be able to achieve first page rankings and top results.

SEO is a legitimate practice that helps websites to generate higher rankings on search engine results, however there are many illegitimate companies claiming to be trustworthy SEO agencies that have given the industry a bad reputation by providing aggressive tactics and attempting to get one over on the search engines ultimately resulting in damaging the website they are representing.

Google are aware of the scam practices that are out there which is why they implement various updates and algorithms on a regular basis to try and eradicate the bad sites from the good.

Other search engines aren't as brutal in their strictness and algorithm and update implementation as Google, but it's worth bearing in mind that Google has the largest search demographic and as most people use Google, it's refreshing to see that they value the websites that they index and try to support them accordingly with the various updates and algorithms they release, to penalise those sites manipulating the system to try and cheat at ranking.

SEO is the best way to generate online revenue and traffic. As a lot of enquiries and/or purchases are made online, it's imperative now more than ever to ensure you have a visible ranking within the Search Engines in order to tap into the online market and ultimately generate more business. You'll not be able to grow online without this.

Keep reading for more information on SEO advice, procedures and tactics to help you along your way to getting to the top spots of the search engines.

Google's Ranking factors

Google takes many things into consideration before ranking a website for a particular search query. Firstly they break it down into several categories and start by looking at:

Domain factors:

- They check the age of your domain to assess how long you have been within your market;

- They assess whether or not your domain contains any keywords and if it is a TLD or Top Level Domain (see *can your domain impact your Search Engine Optimisation* for more information)

- The registration length of your domain to check your businesses validity. In other words, if you have paid for your domain for several years in advance you will be seen as more authoritative than someone that is perhaps paying for their domain on a rolling monthly basis.

- Exact Match Domains (EMDs), provided it is of a high quality and relevant to the search at hand. For instance if someone searches for Darlington's used cars, and your URL is www.darlingtonsusedcars.co.uk then this is an exact match domain.

- Country TLD extensions help you to rank well for searches in that particular country, so with a site ending in .co.uk you'd rank accordingly for UK searches.

-

Page Factors:

- Keywords in your title tags, as if this is relevant to the search it will indicate that your page is relevant.

- Keywords in your description tags – again helping to assess the relevance of your page to the query.

- Content length – the longer and more in-depth your content the better your chances of ranking.

- Keyword density – this you really need to be careful with as if you are looking to be found for a particular keyword or phrase, you don't want to use it too many times within your content so that it looks unnatural as this will lead to search engines penalising you and preventing your site from being found by searchers.

- Page loading speed – the faster your page loads – the better you'll rank – as there is nothing an internet searcher hates more than waiting a long time for a page to load.

- Duplicate content – whether duplicate content may be from another page within your site or another website entirely – it is to be avoided entirely. All content should be unique and relevant to your website to make you stand out. Plagiarising someone else's content will only harm your website.

- Optimising images – ensuring you are utilising all elements of your site for optimisation purposes including your images. Make sure you include tags that are relevant to the image at hand and ultimately that the image is relevant to the content on the page.

- Keywords in your H tags. – You should usually aim to include keywords here and there throughout your <h1> - <h6> tags to further emphasise the relevance of your content.

- User Friendly layout. – If your site is easy to use and access throughout – your users will keep coming back. If it's difficult to work out how to get through then your users won't come back and ultimately Google won't rank you well.

Social Factors:

- Number of tweets and likes – the more people that like your website and interact with you through social channels will impact your search presence.

- Number of Google +1s – again the more popular your website the more seriously you will be taken.

- Social signal relevancy – this is where you can produce content on a regular basis and interact with your user base – so it makes sense to ensure you're entirely relevant through all of your social channels.

How SEO can help your business succeed online

There are many people who claim to be Search Engine Optimisation experts. Most of them however, would struggle to know exactly what you do and don't need to do to get the best rankings on Google and other search engines alike.

Make no mistake, there are many factors that search engines take into consideration when ranking websites. Quite often you'll hear phrases such as *"content is king"* or *"content is nothing without back links"* these phrases aren't entirely inaccurate, but they aren't fully true either.

Google is the search engine that all websites want to dominate. Let's face it, they have the bigger user base so it's no wonder everyone pioneers to get to the top spots. Not many SEO agencies or freelancers would be able to provide you with exact information taken straight out of the Google hand book. Of course with all of their procedures changing regularly and because they release various updates, it's hard to know where to start; but here you can find out quality and relevant information that will help improve your SERPs (Search Engine Ranking Positions).

Google work on various different types of programmes that they call *"rating programmes"*. These rating programmes cover various factors that monitor all indexed websites to rank them accordingly. These factors cover all areas of a website such as content, links and page quality.

Here it's imperative to tell you about all the areas behind SEO including Page Quality Rating, Keyword research and implementation, Panda, Penguin, Pigeon and Hummingbird as well as what areas of your website the search engines take into consideration when ranking you. But more importantly how users view your website and the relevance of their query to your site and the information/products/services you provide.

Before you attempt to implement the best possible SEO strategy to your site, you should know one key factor. Many people try to get around Google by finding shortcuts and illegitimate tactics to get them to the top. As a result they get penalised and struggle to rank effectively after. Google isn't looking for quick time champions; it'll reward you for having a natural online presence, great authority, reliability, a trusted community and interaction with your customers. Of course word of mouth (social mentioning's, likes, followers and engagement as well as backlinks) helps them to rank you higher as well.

What are Page Quality Ratings?

Page Quality Ratings or PQ for short is a rating requirement Google look for that consists of taking a URL and a number of questions that are ultimately designed to accurately guide visitors through your site through the associated landing page to the URL.

Page quality ratings essentially evaluate how well your website can achieve its intended purpose. All websites and Webpages have different purposes and intentions and Google has different expectations and standards for different types of pages as they understand no two pages are necessarily the same.

Google look for many things when optimising websites that most SEO agencies are unaware of. Page quality ratings are derived by Google employees that user their own experience of using the web as an ordinary user in their "*rating locale*". Essentially what this means is that you will be given a page rating based on the ease of use of your website and how your website functions in relation to its targeted guidelines.

Page quality ratings are often over looked as an essential practice in SEO. This is because a lot of agencies and marketers are unable to see the value of the functionality of a website and the overall result it can have with the intended user(s).

Think of it this way. Would you buy from an ecommerce site that didn't look very nice and was difficult to navigate? The answer is probably not. Take a look at some great industry leaders such as Amazon and eBay. These sites have an easy functionality to them that makes it very easy for users to get to where they are looking to go.

Be sure to put yourself in your user's shoes. Can you easily find what you are looking for? Is everything laid out in an understandable manner? If not, then you know you need to make some changes. Less is quite often more and you need to ensure your target demographics will have great success navigating your site.

This may not sound like imperative SEO advice or SEO info, but it is certainly a definitive starting point. On its own it won't have a significant impact on your search results but it should help to increase your conversion rate and lower your bounce rate.

SEO is not an exact science and it is a very intricate forever updating process, so you need to ensure all of your bases are covered in order to get the best SERPs.

Understanding different kinds of websites and Webpages

Page Quality Rating requires an extensive understanding of websites. Google doesn't employ people that don't know what they are talking about. Their procedures are extensive and thorough for a reason. Results! Ultimately they want you to keep using their search engine so they want to provide you with the best answers possible.

Some of you may be thinking a website is a website and that they're all the same. You couldn't be wrong. Your website will be indexed according to the category it falls under.

Search Engines:
There are **search engines** and directories. These websites serve a particular purpose to their intended users, typically that they are looking for something.

Informational:
Then there are **informational** types of websites. Surely that's all websites? This category is typically used for news websites such as BBC or CNN and can extend as far as Wikipedia and encyclopaedia type website.

Personal:
Then you get **personal** websites. We all know someone with a personal website, whether they are using it to showcase their portfolio or just generally showcase information that is personal to them.

Blogs and Diary Sites:
Following on from personal websites you get **blogs** and diary sites. These are sites that are essentially public

diaries sharing your thoughts and information with the world as you know it.

Forums:
Then come the **forums**. These websites are similar to blogs and search engines whereby people post questions or thoughts in the hopes of receiving comments answers and feedback.

Company websites:
Then there are **company** websites. This is where you can find out information of a company of a particular kind that is typically an information site with various Calls to Action encouraging you to phone or email them.

Ecommerce websites:
These are not to be confused with **ecommerce** websites. These are online shops where you can purchase items over the internet. These differ from company websites as their products/services are available to be purchased on their site.

Web 2.0 websites:
Then come the **Web 2.0** websites. These sites can vary in their offerings. These can be platforms in which you can build other websites, or file platforms where you can create documents without having to download software. These websites are the ones that a step above the rest in certain elements.

Social Networking Sites:
You then get the **social networking** websites. These are platforms where people post pictures of themselves, connect with their friends and communicate with one another. If you're not aware what a social network is, you may want to rethink your visit to this site.

File Sharing:
You also get **file sharing** websites. These are sites
where you can store all of your documents as a backup
or if your storage capacity on your laptop/pc is not large
enough for the volume of data you need to store. Easily
accessible and convenient for many.

Different types of websites are indexed in different ways.
Be sure you know the type of website you have before
trying to optimise it as another. The type of website you
have will also determine how Google categorise you in
SEO and how you are represented.

Understanding the Webpage Categories

Websites are typically a group of Webpages containing links to other pages to connect them all together. Websites can be made by individuals, companies, educational institutions, government bodies or any kind of organisation. Wikipedia, YouTube, Facebook ad Yahoo are popular examples of websites.

However, websites can also indicate a collection of pages owned and controlled by a singular source such as one individual or one business (for example mywebsite.com mywebsite.com/page1 mywebsite.com/page2 and so on). Websites also refer to much larger hosts also such as Google which were created with the intention to archive all websites and use them for search purposes, mail purposes, news and image purposes.

A Webpage is essentially a document that is on the World Wide Web. These pages can be visited with most (not necessarily all depending on software) browsers such as Internet Explorer, Firefox, Chrome, or Safari. In the initial periods of the internet, Webpages were predominantly just text and links.

Today the functionality of Webpages is much greater with content that includes images and videos and various functionality purposes such as email, online shopping and games.

A homepage of a website is typically the page you usually land on, or rather the main page of the sire. There is usually a home link or icon on a website to help direct you to their home page if you are unsure of what a homepage is. A subpage is a page on the same site that is not the home page. So with the example mentioned earlier mywebsite.com would be the home page and mywebsite.com/page1 would be a subpage.

A URL the address you type into a browser to find the website or page you are looking for. Fortunately Google doesn't expect you to know the difference between hosting and domains in order to rank well; otherwise ranking would only be available to a select few.

And whilst we're on the topic of all things website related, you may as well ensure you know what a webmaster is. This is typically the person that designs, develops and maintains a website.

These points may not seem relevant to search engine optimisation or indeed SEO advice, but they are. Providing you have a comfortable understanding of the differences between websites and Webpages along with understanding the differences of certain types of pages, this will better help you optimise your website.

By optimising all pages but ensuring you have a great deal of optimisation strategy to your home page as well, you will see your website as a whole rank and not just particular pages. This is crucial in Google's eyes as they want to see you promoting all areas of your website and not just select pages.

Not the most substantial SEO advice but this info can be of use for future reference, and you always need to ensure you've got your bases covered before setting off into the complicated territory of SEO.

What purpose do Webpages serve?

Each webpage has a different purpose. It's usually fairly explanatory, whether it was written for informative purposes or indeed for business purposes the method is usually clear. The purpose of a page is important in determining the Page Quality Rating. This is achieved by assessing how well the page achieves its purpose. They should be created to help users.

As long as the page is set out to help users with what they came to the site looking for then a high PQ rating will be given. But there is no reason you cannot utilise this to suit your own needs with SEO purposes. Ensure the words/phrases you want to be found for are present on your pages/site. So long as it is relevant to the page you are writing it on then you will not be penalised at all.

Ensure you use terminology that your demographic will understand and be sure to utilise the best keyword strategy possible. This does not constitute using the same word or phrase over and over again in the hopes of gaining better authority for that word or phrase as you will be penalised for doing so. Why? Because that is not natural. Google rewards the natural. This will be a recurring theme.

If your website/business covers multiple areas, then you do not need to ensure each page mentions each area, just keep it natural. Page 1 content can include information about the page 1 services you offer. Page 2 content can include information about the page 2 services you offer and so on. The home page is where you can mention multiple services but not always all.

Avoid sounding spammy and ensure your site is comprehensible. If nothing else to keep visitors coming back. You want to be seen as authoritative and informative whilst also professional and clear. You can't be any of these if you over use your keywords and phrases making your site spammy. This will not work in your favour for ranking or ultimately generating business.

You can utilise each and every page on your website for your SEO potential and services. Ensure you are giving visitors a reason to come back. Make sure your content makes sense and is distributed evenly throughout the site. This is not as easy as it sounds and there are various procedures you need to ensure you stick to.

Pages that have an impact on user's health or wealth

Google refers to pages that can impact your health, happiness or wealth of potential users as Your Money or Your Life (YMYL) Pages. This is handy to understand particularly when it comes to their ranking in search engine optimisation. These pages are typically:

- Payment pages
- Financial information pages
- Medical information pages
- Legal information pages
-

To explore in more detail, these can be pages such as payment pages like shops, online banking or bill payments. Financial information pages, such as credit rating pages, tax information pages, mortgage advice page or insurance pages.

Medical information pages are pages such as online doctor diagnosis pages, information on treating ailments or diseases, nutritional information pages and so on. Then you get the legal information pages. These are sites that will contain legal advice about various areas of law. But these are not the definitive set of "your money or your life" pages. Essentially it is left down to the people at Google to use their own discretion when labelling a website.

If you have an YMYL page, then it's good news for you. When it comes to optimising these websites, search engines take them very seriously.

If your site has information or products on it that could significantly improve the happiness, health or wealth of your users then you will be ranked very well with a high Page Quality Rating providing you fall into line with all of the other requirements Google sets out.

If you have a malicious version of a YMYL website and you're looking to negatively impact your users happiness, health or wealth then watch out because you will be penalised by the Search Engine masters and you're Page Quality Rating will be extremely low.

Needless to say, if you're a malicious organisation and you're looking to exploit users that come to your site be it through search engines or not, you will not be rewarded with high Page Quality Ratings or indeed rankings. Good luck ever trying to get a site like this onto the first 20 pages of the biggest search engines.

You'll notice a steady theme from this. Google is a business and like all business it wants to provide the best possible experience to its users in order to keep them coming back.

Google wants to be your friend and put the right search results your way. It will always work on being a better search engine than it is, but for the most part, people are very impressed with Google. If they weren't, Google wouldn't be as big as it is today, and nor would the search market.

This SEO advice will come in handy for any YMYL websites, providing you with SEO information and advice to help expand your current knowledge of the search market.

SEO and what you should know in summary

There are many things you need to take into consideration in order to rank in the search engines, but if you aren't able to get the on page basics right then you're probably not going to rank very well at all.

When it comes to competitive keywords or phrases, you will be virtually non-existent to the search engine market. It's also worth noting that if you have the best off page SEO strategy but a poor on site strategy that won't work in your favour. You need to show that you mean business and that you deserve a place at the top.

A lot of people ignore the basics of SEO and focus predominantly on getting links instead of focusing on what they can change themselves, being the optimisation of their own sites. Make no mistake, on site SEO is the foundation of any SEO campaign.

If you can get it right there's a high chance you'll succeed with your quest on the search engines; but if you get it wrong and don't make your on sight changes, chances are you will never hit the top spots for the key words you are looking to target no matter what work you have accomplished off-page.

We understand that you may not have an extensive knowledge of SEO and how to rank, so here is a step by step guide to getting your on-page SEO right. We'll cover the basics as well as the more intricate processes that you will need in place in order to hit the top spots and ultimately beat your online competitors.

It's also worth mentioning that because SEO is constantly evolving, you should ensure these processes are all up-to-date and keep up with any changing regulations and recommendations the search engines make.

- **Make sure your site is device friendly.**

  This sounds very obvious, but so many sites aren't utilising this tactic to encourage visitors from multiple devices. Always aim to ensure you have a responsive version of your site so that it will resize according to each device it is visited from.

  This will make your users so much happier saving them time from having to zoom in and scroll across to read the infinite amount of text or search your products. Ensuring your site is mobile friendly will not only expand your demographic, but it will also show you are considerate of your users' needs which the search engines love to see.

  The world has come a long way since the introduction of the search engines and a substantial amount of us use various devices to the point where many organisations are claiming mobile usage will surpass desktop usage as early as next year. Ensuring your site can respond to multiple devices can only work in your favour, so it's worth implementing.

- **Content.**

  You may have spoken to many agencies or SEO gurus that claim content is king. The truth is content counts for a huge amount of what Google look for when it comes to ranking.

A great way to prove this is by looking at Google's Panda update. This algorithm ensures that gone are the days of being able to get away with bleak or irrelevant content and that you should be focusing your efforts on creating unique and most importantly informative content.

Content runs a little bit deeper than just being unique though, you have to ensure your content has been written for your users as that's who you should be writing it for. A lot of sites are written to try to please the search engines, and for a while that worked, but now it doesn't. They're crawling your site to ensure your content is written for your users first and the search engines second so be sure to keep this in mind. Just make sure that with this you are able to include your key phrases and words in a natural flowing way that makes sense to your readers, and don't include them in every sentence on every line. It won't do you any favours.

This brings us on to keyword stuffing that makes no sense anymore, so if you're doing it, you really don't deserve to rank well. Google's algorithm works on assessing semantics. So it will be able to tell if you are writing about your topic naturally and that your content is relevant. So long as you ensure your content is unique, under no circumstances copied from somewhere else and natural flowing, you should be fine.

This information is useful, but you need to be mindful of the message(s) you want to convey and keep that at the forefront of all the content you produce. Your content should sell and drive leads whilst building brand awareness and inform your target demographic. Finally, be sure to get it checked before you post it. What may look great to you may not be so great to someone else so be sure to ask for an additional perspective.

- **Meta Descriptions**

  It used to be that rankings heavily depended on Meta descriptions of sites, but in truth they don't contribute to Search Engine Ranking Positions (SERPs) much anymore. However, they are still an important part of on-page optimisation.

  These descriptions are the first introduction potential visitors get from your brand so it will work in your favour to get them right. These should be well written and around 156 characters in length. Try and make this as informative as possible and don't miss out on the opportunity to make this a small sales pitch. Don't spam or over optimise these descriptions and ensure this makes sense to the users as well as the search engines.

- **Title Tags**

  Here you need to ensure you place your main keywords and phrases and their attributed variations in the title tags. Don't try to trick search engines by using the same keyword for each page. This won't help you or your business.

  Ensure your title tags are written in a natural way which incorporates your focused keyword or phrase. It used to be that Google would display around 70 characters of title tags but now since developing they display based on pixel width so there is no set number for how long title tags should be. Keep it short and sweet, yet relevant and natural.

Don't keyword stuff or put spammy content in your title tags. Nobody likes them and it won't help you.

- **Heading tags**

  H tags! You should be using H tags in a strategic way across all of your pages. H1 tags – be sure you utilise headings accurately without keyword stuffing them and over doing it. H1 tags should consist of your main keyword (or phrase) making sure it works for users and then the search engines. H2 tags come next and this is when you should focus on your secondary keywords and follow suit for H3 tags and so on.

  Be sure to only use one H1 tag per page as you can use H2-H6 tags multiple times.

  Vary your keywords in each heading tag. These will enhance the value of your content and makes it easier to read for both users and search bots. Heading tags effectively signal the importance of the headings on your site so you need to be accurate with where you put your keywords and their attributed variations. Avoid keyword stuffing and over optimising at all costs. This will be detrimental to your ranking aspirations.

- **Robots.txt Files.**

  You can find your robots.txt file located at www.mydomain.com/robots.txt. You may need to consult a web developer if you're unsure how to amend this, but understand you will have to ensure your robots.txt file is in order as this can help you make sure that pages within your sire are being blocked from being crawled by search engines. If your pages are blocked from being crawled then you cannot rank those pages for their attributed keywords which puts all the other onsite effort you've made out of the window.

If you see disallow:/ followed by any page name or directory on your site, you need to assess whether or not that page should be accessible to search engines. If you're unsure the best practice to go by is to block admin panels and low quality pages to your site which need to be in place for your overall structure and performance but you don't want the search engines to index them. If you see a page that is of value to your site being disallowed then make sure you take it out.

This process is fundamental in order to rank well. Whether you need extensive SEO advice or not – robots.txt info is valid to all websites. Make sure you've got yours set up correctly.

- **Canonicalization of duplicate content.**

After Panda, being picked up on content duplication is one of the worst things you can be penalised for. Its common practice for most CMS's (Content Management Systems) to allow pages to be accessible via a number of different URLs. This is bad news for sites looking to rank well. In these cases, these sites are looking to manipulate search engines and the results by having a page live on a duplicate URL. If you do have this, you should be ok in adding a canonical tag to reference the page for Google to index instead of indexing both. Google with then attribute Page Rank to this page and not both.

If you're unsure of how to do this, then go to Google directly for information on implementing canonicalization. It isn't that time consuming, and it's worth spending a few minutes to get your head around the process rather than having to reproduce content for all duped pages.

This should be one of the first things you implement as it is of significant importance to your Search Engine Ranking Positions, your Page Quality and indeed your overall SEO behaviour.

- **Page Speed**

    If you're unsure about the strength of your page speed then ask Google. Sounds ridiculous, but they have many tools available in order to help you maximise your online potential. You can check you Page Speed by Google's developers themselves. This will help you outline how fast they are able to load your site as well as providing you with a vast selection of suggestions to show how you can improve things. It's best to get your score higher than 90. This helps to ensure you're not a Search Engine Ranking Position lower than you should be because your site is slow.

    You may not think page speed is that important, but market research indicates the longer your site takes to load, the sooner the user will get bored and look somewhere else. It's happened to all of us, and not everyone is patient.

- **Crawl error resolutions:**

    Always be sure to check your Webmaster tools for crawl errors on your site in order to find a way to rectify and errors that may be showing. Crawl errors aren't great for anybody be it users or search engines, but fortunately they are pretty easy to sort out with 301 redirects if they are removed pages or 302 redirects if they have only been removed temporarily.

You have to use a lot of common sense when it comes to deciding where you are going to redirect to. Don't redirect to another page just for the sake of it ensure you are redirecting to the relevant alternative. If you don't have a relevant alternative to redirect to then you'll have to implement a redirect to a 404 page instead.

- **Structure of URLs.**

  Some sites use query strings for page URLs which is something that needs to be changed. If you have the opportunity, ensure your links are search engine friendly. This makes it easier for both search engines and users to understand. If your instance you had www.mydomain.com/page-name then it's easy to assess what that page will be about rather than www.mydomain.com/index.php?id=1. This makes no sense to users and search engines as this doesn't say what the page is about or give you any chance of targeting it for a potential keyword. This should be one of your first priorities with onsite work. Ensure you break out of the standardised URL structures that nobody likes as it will benefit your site performance.

  Try to avoid the use of underscores as search engines much prefer hyphens. With this, it's also imperative to ensure you implement 301 redirects from the old URL to the new one should you have to make any changes, or else you'll be presented with crawl errors in your Webmaster Tools and your users will be face with 404 error pages.

Hopefully you should now have a better understanding of the onsite changes that have to be implemented in order to rank well. On-site SEO is imperative in reaching the top spots and if you're able to do it yourself, it also helps saving the cost of a web developer charging you for it.

Page titles explained

Be sure to create unique and accurate page titles to each page of your site.

Page titles serve a purpose to both users and search engines. They help to indicate the topic of the page and what information and/or services/products will be available on that page. Title tags should be placed within the head tag of the HTML document behind the site. Each page to your website should have a unique title. An example of a great Page title is highlighted below:

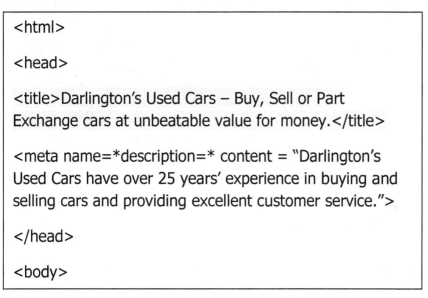

```
<html>

<head>

<title>Darlington's Used Cars – Buy, Sell or Part
Exchange cars at unbeatable value for money.</title>

<meta name=*description=* content = "Darlington's
Used Cars have over 25 years' experience in buying and
selling cars and providing excellent customer service.">

</head>

<body>
```

This website title clearly indicates the company name and its business areas to help ensure it is put in front of relevant traffic searching for buying, selling or part exchanging cars.

What's more with page titles, is that they are displayed in search results as a description to the website. With any website that ranks on search engines, the contents of the title tag of the page that has been listed will appear in the search results. The titles are hyperlinked taking you to the site that is listed and the description underneath, in summary is there to help users establish if that site is relevant to the search that they made.

Google   used cars darlington

Web   Maps   Images   Shopping   News   More ▼   Search tools

About 617,000 results (0.74 seconds)

Darlington's Used Cars: Buy, Sell or Part Exchange ...
www.darlingtonsusedcars.co.uk ▼
Darlington's Used Cars have over 25 years' experience in buying and selling cars and providing excellent customer service.

How to ensure you're doing it right

- **Be sure you accurately describe the content on that page.**

Avoid using a title that bears no relation to the page or the content within the page.

Don't use default or non-descript titles like "Page 1" as this will provide no insight to the search engines nor the searchers and your potential users.

- **Ensure each page has a unique title**

By creating unique titles for each of your pages, you are able to better identify the differences of each of the pages on your site, which in turn helps the search engines rank you better, and helps to understand the flow of your site.

Don't use the same title tag on all of your pages as this will confuse the search engines and you're not providing information to indicate the different pages of your website.

- **Don't go overboard, be clear and concise.**

Your titles should be brief and descriptive. If your title is too long only a portion of it will be available to read in search results. Typically you should aim to keep your title between 50 and 60 characters. Your title should be helpful and useful, rather than lengthy and useless.

Whatever you do don't keyword stuff. You have to bear in mind potential visitors to your site will see your title in search – think of what it would have to look like in order for you to click on it.

Page titles are an important part of search engine optimisation, so you need to be sure you get it right.

Using "Description" Meta tags

As well as assigning titles to each page of your website, you are also able to provide a short description of each page in order to summarise what your page is about. A lot of businesses and individuals struggle to accurately convey the page in a short description especially when the given guideline is 150-160 characters. Google have recognised this and provide some expert solutions to your problems with their content analysis tool. These are particularly handy to implement as your description tag is shown in organic listings on search engines.

Description tags are implemented in your HTML head beneath your title tag. Here is a great example of a Meta description:

```
<html>

<head>

<title>Darlington's Used Cars – Buy, Sell or Part Exchange cars at
unbeatable value for money.</title>

<meta name=*description=* content = "Darlington's Used Cars have
over 25 years' experience in buying and selling cars and providing
excellent customer service.">

</head>

<body>
```

And you can see how your Meta description is displayed in search results:

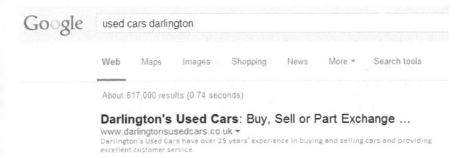

These description tags help to further summarise what that page in your website involves and how it is it relevant to the query a user has searched. This allows search engines and users to better assess the relevance of your website to the enquiry that has been made.

How to do it right:

- **Provide an accurate summary of what is on the page.**

Here it is imperative to write a description to gain the interest of the user whilst informing them of the information you are providing.

It would be entirely useless to write a description that was of no relevance to the page at hand, just as using a generic description would be. Having a description such as "page about cars" would be of little to no use to prospective visitors, so be sure to be accurate.

It's also best to provide natural descriptions and avoid utilising all key words you are hoping to be found for as this will look spammy and ultimately drive people away from your site. Keep it separate from the content that may already be on the page, and just guide the user through what they may find.

- **Each page must have a unique description.**

Like title tags, each page's description must be unique to the page at hand. No two pages should be the same on your site so be sure this is adequately reflected within the description.

Understanding the relevance of URL Structures

If your URL is easy to understand it will help to convey the information of your site more easily. Think of your URL and each page within it as a filing system. It needs to make sense and be easy to understand in order to best find what you are looking for. As well as the structure of your URL keeping your site more organised, it can also mean search engines are able to crawl your site more effectively based on the simple organisation of your URL structure.

What's more, for any site that wants to link back to yours, it will look clear and concise and not like spam, therefore encouraging other sites to link to you. If you were to be presented with a long, confusing and ultimately cryptic URL and you were unsure of the relevance to the content you were reading, you have to ask yourself if you'd be likely to click it. Providing your links are easy to understand and to the point – you should receive no hesitation in visitors clicking through to your site from other variables.

URLs that are confusing and not user friendly can look something like this:

Users would struggle to recite this for future reference and would struggle to link back to it effectively. The URL is also very long and users may not read it. With a URL like this, having parameters that are not easily recognisable run the risk of not being used correctly.

If the URL contains words that are relevant to the content within the page and site, this enables users and search engines alike to have a greater insight into the information within the page that a folder name and number would not.

With results that appear in search engines, relevant words are highlighted in bold as shown below:

Darlington's Used Cars: Buy, Sell or Part Exchange ...
www.darlingtonsusedcars.co.uk ▾
Darlington's Used Cars have over 25 years' experience in buying and selling cars and providing excellent customer service.

The words of relevance will appeal more to a user than the ID number as previously listed. Search engines can crawl any kinds of URLs no matter how complex they may seem, but it certainly helps to find URLs that are as simple as possible for users and search engines alike. This can be achieved by rewriting dynamic URLs to static URLs. This is an advanced procedure that is best left to webmasters, but the procedure needs to be done correctly, as otherwise you will cause errors to your site leading to issues with being able to index your site correctly.

How to do it correctly:

- Ensure you use words in your URL. Providing the words are relevant to your content and the structure of your URLs are user friendly and help to better organise your site to users and search engines, visitors will remember your URL better and will be more willing to link to your site. Ensure your links aren't unnecessarily lengthy and try to avoid using parameter IDs. Avoid keeping page titles generic and using excessive amounts of keywords

- Create a simple structure for your site. By sing a directory style structure, you are organising your website well and it makes it easier for users and search engines to know where they are going on your site. By using a directory structure you are able to better indicate the type of information available on each given page. Avoid having multiple subdirectories as this can cause confusion to potential users, and ensure you keep the directory names of the site relevant to the pages and the information on them.

Ensure you have high quality content, information and services.

If you are able to produce high quality content and information on your website you will increase your online recognition without having to do anything extra. Creating unique and insightful content will help influence your site drastically.

Other factors such as URLs, title and description tags all weigh in, but without unique content and information, you wouldn't rank well at all on the search engines. Users know good content, contrary to what some sites out there might tell you. With good content comes great publicity.

If someone sees your information and realises they know of people that would benefit from it – they will share it through their social media accounts or their blogs and forums or indeed through email or instant messaging. The ways in which users can share your content is vast – but it's worthwhile implementing buttons on your site to encourage this behaviour.

Organic boosting (or online word of mouth to put it simply) is what will help your site to rank well within all the search engines. Why? It's relevant, its informative, it's trusted and it's popular If your site s popular it must therefore be reputable. If it is reputable it must therefore be trustworthy. If it is trustworthy it must therefore be providing adequate up-to-date information to its users. This is a valued aspect to any business, and it should be no different for online strategies and tactics. Think of it this way, if a website didn't have great quality content and useful information and services would it be shared and recommended so frequently online? The answer is glaringly obvious, as it should be to any marketer.

One thing to bear in mind in any focus of your business, is how your users interpret the information you provide. Different people perceive things in different ways, so it's worthwhile anticipating the different understandings users may generate from your content so be sure you are as clear and concise as possible to avoid possible misinterpretation.

Sadly there is no fool proof way to ensure nobody misreads your information, but you can lower the number significantly provided you offer clear explanations, unique USPs (Unique Selling Points), clear KPIs (Key Performance Indicators) and informative information as to what you offer and provide on your website. To do this effectively, think about how your market may search for you.

This sounds easier than it seems as they may not be typing in industry specific keywords and phrases, they may just be searching for generic terminology so you need to ensure you are covering all possible bases. It is important to remember here that the businesses or individuals that are looking for your website will not be experts in your industry – that is meant to be you after all.

Through anticipation of these differences in behaviours from your potential intended search demographic, can help to produce positive results from the traffic you acquire online. You can look into this further by analysing the keyword market and discovering what people are searching for within your industry.

With the Darlington's Used Cars as an example, you may want to target the term "*gifts*" at the risk of generating generic traffic that isn't looking to explore the used car industry. By focusing on more specific keywords such as "*blue car gifts*" or "*gifts for cars*" are not only more relevant to what the business is offering, it is also preventing erroneous traffic from reaching your site and increasing your bounce rate as you are not what they are looking for.

Great ways to ensure you generate the most traffic and retain a good portion of the market is to be up-to-date, competitive and exciting. You can do this by providing research on your industry that other business don't, you could provide survey findings and emphasise why you offer what you offer.

To be the most relevant to your searchers you need to write content that is easy to understand. Searchers enjoy unique content that is well written and easy to follow. Avoid writing boring content with grammatical and vocabulary errors.

Be sure to stay organised and coherent. Readers like to know where they will start reading and where they will finish reading. Some users want to find specific piece of information so it may be in your best interests to devise your content into blocks so that it's easier to access and summarise. Avoid writing mass amounts of text on each page without clearly heading or subheading varying sections or using any form of separation.

The importance of unique content on a regular basis not only helps to keep your frequent customers coming back, it also helps to generate new visitors. At all costs, avoid duplicating anyone else's content as this will cause your website to be penalised and slim your chances form ever being effectively indexed on the search engines.

This content will bring no value to your intended market so don't use it, create your own. As well as this, avoid having the same content published on multiple pages throughout your site as this will cause the same damaging issues. You need to ensure all content throughout you site is unique and indeed relevant to each page.

Your content should primarily be aimed at your users and not at search engines. So long as your content is coherent and makes sense to your users you will be able to rank better within the search engines. Many websites try to manipulate their content to best suit the search engines to the detriment of their users. Ensure all text is visible to users as it is best practice to be entirely visible to your users as well as to search engines so as not to pull the wool over either your users or search engines eyes.

The way you write your anchor text will ultimately affect your SERPs

Anchor text is sometimes overlooked when it comes to optimising websites effectively. Here we will cover the use of great anchor text and how it will further impact your search engine optimisation. Having insightful anchor text helps to convey the contents of the page at hand. In order to best understand how anchor text can impact your website, it would help to understand what it is. Anchor text is the text that users will see as a link to click within the content of your website and it is placed within the anchor tag <a href=*_*></a> and will look something like the following:

<a href*http://www.darlingtonsusedcarsales.co.uk/services/cars-for-sale.html>Cars For Sale</a>

This text informs both search engines and users more about the page you are linking to. Whether these links are linking to internal pages within your site, or external links linking to pages outside of your website, it helps to provide content that is informative of where they will be leading.

What to avoid:

- Writing generic anchor text such as "*click here*" or otherwise uninformative text. Anchor text can boost your search engine optimisation providing it uses key words you are looking to optimise around, but primarily is relevant and informative to the link you are connecting to.

- Creating anchor text that is of no relation to the page you are linking to. This process will impede the results you are intending. An example could be "*Used cars for sale*" and linking to a page about "*selling your used car*".

- Writing unnecessarily long anchor text. Be clear and concise.

- Making links look like regular text. They need to be visible to your users to be effective. If users can't see the links you are implementing, they will not be able to reach the intended page you are directing them to.

- Don't stuff keywords into anchor text to try and trick search engines. This will not look natural and search engines will not reward you for doing so, and your users will not appreciate this tactic either.

- Creating links just for the sake of creating links. They should be relevant to the content on the page.

Making effective use of optimising your images

Any decent website will have images that are relevant to the information and/or the services provided. Information can be relayed to images through the "*alt attribute*".

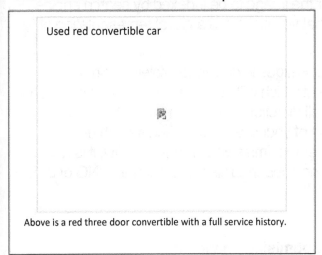

Used red convertible car

Above is a red three door convertible with a full service history.

This information is imperative to the images for several reasons. Firstly, the alt attributes can contribute to your search engine optimisation provided you are able to tag them correctly. Secondly, if a visitor to your site is using an older version of a browser that doesn't support the images, it is worthwhile providing a text caption so that they are able to see some information about what the image should contain as the picture illustrates.

It also provides information to search engine robots that are crawling your site as to what that image contains and how it is relevant to the page and content.

Alt attributes are also useful if you are using the image as a link to another page. This is particularly apparent on ecommerce sites when providing a link to the product with more information on the product. This is treated in the same way as anchor text is treated when linking to another page within the site or a link outside of the site.

When you are providing an alt attribute to an image it also makes it easier for the image to be indexed by search engine image pages so that you can have a visual representation of your content.

You can store your images in directories solely assigned for image management which will help organise your website. This simplifies the overall direction of your site and helps to further simply the direction of your site to users and search engines alike. To help further maximise your image visibility, it is worth ensuring they are on supported file types such as PNG or JPEG format.

The best way of optimising images:

Ensure your alt attributes are short and informative. It also helps to avoid using generic filenames as these will also be indexed on your site, so its worth while ensuring the filename is relevant to the image. Again, provided the filenames are short and informative, it will work better towards the correct optimisation of them. It's also advisable to avoid keyword stuffing in this metric also.

Ensuring the correct use of heading tags

Heading tags are used primarily to structure a page for users. It is important not to confuse heading tags with the <head> HTML tag or indeed the HTTP headers. Heading tags are in six sizes <h1>, <h2>, <h3>, <h4>, <h5> and <h6>. <h1> tags are the most important tags for your page, and decrease in importance down to <h6> tags. An example of what heading tags should look like is as follows:

```
</head>

<body>

<h1>Darlington's Used Cars</h1>

<h2>About Us – We believe in Quality Customer Care</h2>

<p> We understand how difficult searching for the perfect car
can be, so we aim to make the ride as smooth as possible in
helping you find a quality used car to suit your needs and
requirements.</p>
```

Ultimately it is down to you how you use your heading tags, on a page containing multiple sections such as *about us* it could be worth implementing the name of the site or a page primarily into the <h1> tag and the following topics and pieces of information in <h2> and <h3> tags.

Heading tags usually make the text within them appear larger than the rest of the text on the page (as all titles rightly should). This helps inform users that the text is of significant value as can help them further deduce the text that will follow. Using multiple title sizes helps users and search engines to generate the structure of importance of the content on the page. All important information will be listed first with the least important information listed last. Heading tags have to be implemented correctly as they are an imperative part of the overall websites aesthetic functionality. If they are done incorrectly, they run the risk of alienating your audience by looking unprofessional and untidy, so be sure to keep them effective and eye catching.

The best way to compare heading tags on a website and how they should look is comparing them to an academic text book. If you have a chapter title and various subtitles and headings as part of the chapter, these would not be the same size as the title that was listed initial introducing the chapter.

Put some thought behind what you want each title to include and what messages you are looking to convey through these titles. Whatever you do, avoid placing unnecessary text in heading tags as this will be of little to no use to your users and won't effectively help to structure the page(s) at hand. Only use heading tags where appropriate and not in place of other tags such as <strong> tags (HTML tags that convey a strong emphasis of the text at hand) where they will be more appropriate than <h1>-<h6> tags. Be sure to follow the tagging system correctly also and don't drastically move from <h1> tags to <h6> and then randomly convey the other tags in between. You want to make sure your site looks clean and professional and this will not help you do so.

Heading tags should also be used when required and not for every other line. Too many heading tags run the risk of making it unnecessarily difficult for users to scan your website to find the information they are looking for. Heading tags should be used for structural purposes of the page ad not for the design element. Heading tags are exactly what they say they are – headings. They should not be incorporated unnecessarily where they do not serve a purpose.

Understanding the importance of robots.txt

In some instances you can prevent search engine bots from searching and indexing your site, and you can do this by using robotos.txt. A robots.txt file instructs search engines as to whether or not they can access and indeed crawl your site or parts of it. This file must be names "*robots.txt*" and should be placed within the root directory of your site. All search engines will not access the content provided within the robots.txt files, and should look something like this:

```
User-agent: *

Disallow: /images/

Disallow: /search
```

You may choose certain pages of your site to not be indexed because they may not be useful to your users if discovered from a search engine. If you do feel as though preventing search engines from indexing particular pages from your site, you can find various robots.txt generators online to help you create this file within your site. Alternatively, be sure to make your web developer aware of your intent for robots.txt so it can be implemented effectively. It is important noting that if your site uses sub domains and there are pages within a sub domain you do not wish to be indexed, you will have to create a separate robots.txt file for this sub domain.

You can test which URLs search engines can and can't access on your site through various tools, including the robots.txt Tester provided by Google. There are limits to robots.txt, and it is worth being completely aware of these before deciding to or not to implement the robots.txt file, as you may wish to implement another mechanism to prevent your page(s) from being crawled by the search engines.

Downsides to robots.txt file:

- Information

The rules stated in the robots.txt files are not necessarily rules that every crawler must follow. It is better to view the robotos.txt file as a set of guidelines to the search engines. Search engine bots and crawlers will usually obey the commands laid out within the robotos.txt files but other more outdated crawlers may not. You must therefore be aware of the consequences of sharing this information that you intended to not make available. If you have private information that you do not want to make available, you can use other methods to ensure it is not found.

- Reference

While search engines won't crawl or index the pages blocked by your robots.txt file it may be possible to find and index the information on these pages from other websites that may be linking to it. You can stop your URL appearing completely in search results by using your robots.txt file along with other blocking methods such as password protection implemented on these files.

You can implement other methodologies to prevent the crawling and indexing of particular pages by adding the "NOINDEX" tags to you robots.txt files including the Meta tag. It would be worthwhile using more secure methods for anything that may be information sensitive or confidential, as there is still a possibility that search engines can reference what you are trying to prevent from being found. It's worth documenting that there are non-compliant search engines albeit not in as great of use as the more popular search engines, but these will not follow the exclusions put in place by robotos.txt files. Encrypting this information or password protecting it is certainly a more secure alternative.

Being found with mobile optimisation

With mobile usage ever increasing in popularity, it is now imperative to notify Google of your mobile ready site. Ensuring the correct configuration of mobile sites so they are able to be indexed correctly should be one of your top priorities for your site.

Mobile usage is increasing desktop usage for all areas of internet access including search. Mobile sites use a different format than desktop sites and the management of these sites and the attributed expertise is quite different. Fortunately, some CMS (Content Management Systems) such as WordPress and Drupal provide many mobile compatible theme systems making mobile optimisation that much easier. However, with the different formats attributed to mobile compatible sites, it makes it that much harder to find them on search engines as these formats were not designed with search in mind.

Some important tips to help you ensure your site can be optimised for mobile use:

- **Verify your mobile site is indexed by Google**

    Googlebot may not be able to find your site, and if it cannot find your site, it will not be able to index it. You can ensure success by creating a mobile sitemap and submitting it to Google to ensure they are aware that your site exists. Ensuring that your mobile site is recognised by Google (and other search engines) means mobile searchers will be able to find it.

- **Access may be restricted to Googlebot**

Some mobile sites refuse access to search engines and anything else other than mobile devices making it impossible to optimise for mobile use. You can ensure Googlebot can access your site by enabling it in your HTML.

Once you have enabled search engines to crawl your mobile URLs they then check your site to see whether each URL is mobile compatible. If there are sites that aren't mobile compatible they will not be included within the mobile site index; this isn't to say however that they will not be included in the regular desktop index. Provided your site is of a compatible format, the page will be utilised on mobile search. It should look something like this:

```
<!DOCTYPE html PUBLIC *-//WAPFOLUM/DTD XHTML
Mobile
1.0//EN**http://www.wapfolum.org/DTD/xhtml-
mobile10.dtd*>

<html.xmlns*http://www.w3.org/1999/xhtml*>
```

As well as ensuring the mobile optimisation of your site, it is without question that you should ensure you are able to guide mobile users accurately, just as you would desktop users.

It can be difficult running both a mobile and a desktop version of your site, and one of the problems often presented to webmasters that run mobile and desktop versions of a site s ensuring the mobile site appears on mobile devices and the desktop site appears on desktop devices.

You don't want to present a desktop user with a mobile version of your site just as you wouldn't want to present a mobile user with a desktop version of your site. You can ensure this doesn't happen by redirecting mobile users and search bots to the mobile version of your site. Search engines predominantly notice the relationship between the two versions of the sites and will fundamentally display the standard version of the site for desktop users and the mobile version for mobile users. In some instance you may need to redirect mobile users to the mobile version of your site (when they type in the URL for instance) but for search it should not be necessary to redirect users that find you on search you're your mobile site.

SEO Facts and Figures

91% of Internet users use search engines every month

Hardly surprising that over 90% of internet users use search for their queries. This is why it is imperative to optimise your site for search in order to put yourself in front of new business as search engines are how they come to look for it. If they can't see you on their search then they won't find out about you.

The top 5 results get around 75% of the clicks

The first five results (being the top half of page one) generate three quarters of the search traffic. You can't afford to be in the bottom half of page one or even on page two as traffic just doesn't go this far back. You need to be in the top 5 in order to be noticed for what you are optimising for.

Ensure you focus on a few select keywords rather than many as you need to build authority for the select terms in order to get the majority of the traffic.

75% of SEO is off-site and 25% is on-site

You can improve your SEO by off-site and on-site methods. You will need both methods in order to rank sufficiently. Onsite activities include content, URL structure, Title tags and Meta Descriptions whereas off-site consists of link generating, social activity and PR. You need to make sure you focus your time according with your SEO development. 75% off-site and 25% on-site.

Meta descriptions under 155 characters increase CTR

The Meta description is the brief description that shows up below the link on search engines. This gives users a potential idea of what they will get if they click. Therefore it is without question that an enticing Meta description will increase Click Through Rates.

Due to the 155 character limitation you have to ensure that your meta description is short and sweet yet clear and concise.

Google+ is the highest correlated social network for SEO ranking

Social Media presence now plays a huge part in SERPs. As they are a primary form of online communication for most individuals, search engines factor in your social network activity to you SERPs.

One way to utilise this to your advantage is to connect with people who are influential on the phrases you are looking to rank for. If they are able to like, share or +1 your content it will be more likely to show up for other users.

Google + is the second most popular social network, so it's worth utilising Google+ to your advantage.

Is your SEO agency hurting your website?

SEO agencies are trusted to be doing a good job for your site. But would you know if they were actually causing you more harm than good? An alarming number of SEO agencies use black hat tactics that will have a hugely negative impact on your site. Nobody wants this.

You need to be mindful of many things to assess whether or not your SEO agency is actually harming your site. You should find out what these agencies are doing especially during the first few months of your contract. The sooner you can establish what they are doing, the sooner you can assess whether or not they are causing you more harm than good.

There are many warning signs:

Firstly, **they have nothing to show you**. SEO agencies should have something to show. This doesn't have to be with regards to your rankings results, but they should be able to show you the practices they use.

SEO is a lengthy process so you shouldn't be alarmed if you're not seeing results four months in to your campaign. Ensure you get some concrete answers so they can show you where they are spending your money each month. It may be on-site or off site changes but ask them to show you something!

A few months can be a fair while to wait though, so you should be mindful of some things they can offer you if not before your campaign but at the very beginning of any work they do for you. They should be able to show you things such as an SEO audit of your site, an analysis of your link profile, how you optimise your content currently or showing you articles linking back to your site. They could provide a greater insight in this time – but these are some things you should be on the lookout for. Just make sure they can actual prove they are doing work for you.

Another sign of a bad agency is: **they don't ask you for anything!**

SEO agencies aren't miracle workers. An agency that knows what they are talking about will need your help in part. They may require access to your CMS, it's most likely they'll ask for access to your Google Analytics and Webmaster Tools, they may ask for access to your social accounts, what keywords you would like to target and whether or not you have received any audits in the past or if indeed you have been penalised. If you're asked for any or all of these then chances are you're working with a reputable company.

If they don't ask you for anything this could suggest that they are only adding links from link farms to your site from spammy entities. They won't need access to any of the aforementioned practices and the work that they will be implementing is probably very harmful to your site.

If they **have no suggestions for improvements** avoid them at all costs.

Any half decent SEO agency will be able to steer you in the right direction with advice and suggestions. If they are not telling you or asking you to do certain things then this isn't a good sign. It means that they are either putting malicious tactics into your site or they aren't doing anything at all.

If you are working with a reputable SEO agency they will value their relationship with you, they will be honest and informative and you'll have to work with them as they'll make recommendations and suggestions on improving your overall performance.

But what if you ask them what they are doing and **they skirt around the question and try and avoid answering?**

If you've asked them what they're doing and they come back with responses such as *"our work on your behalf must remain confidential"* (why?! You're paying them for a service you should know what service that is!)

"Due to the nature of SEO we can't disclose our methodologies." (Oh so your dentist shouldn't tell you that you need a filling he should just give you one without you knowing?).

"We do many things but ultimately it boils down to improving your ranking on search engines." (Of course you know this you just want to know how they are doing it – you haven't asked an impossible question).

Or a personal favourite *"oh lots of things – it would take too long to explain!"* (Force them to!).

If your agency is skirting over any question you ask to show work that they are implementing for you and they can't give you any definitive responses – then you need to get out of there and quickly! If you asked for what you were getting for you money in a shop – they'd tell you. You wouldn't accept *"oh it's a surprise!"* as a response – so why should you except skirting over the question from your SEO agency?

You get a manual penalty. Suffice to say, a penalty is one of the worst things that can happen to your site. If you're working with an agency and you receive a penalty it's too late to rectify it, but you need to be sure it's from work they have implemented to your site. You'll know that you've been penalised as you will receive a Google Webmaster Tools notification or an email message.

Be sure you find out why you've received a penalty and if it has got anything to do with the agency you've hired.

Your rankings drop. Rankings aren't definitive and can vary daily. You shouldn't be alarmed if your rankings vary by a couple of places but if you've dropped significantly then it's usually a sign that the work this agency is putting into your site isn't all that effective. If your agency can't give you a definitive reason to your dropped rankings then it's probably best to stop working with them.

Your traffic drops. If you suddenly notice a huge decrease in traffic to your site, then dodgy SEO work is probably why. This is very bad. Be sure to ask your agency why this is. If it's a seasonal fluctuation then try not to be too alarmed, but if it's not then be sure to ask as many questions as you can.

Ensure that it isn't an algorithm update which may have impacted traffic volumes, and be sure to assess what changes have been made to your site. Don't be afraid to ask for a definitive picture of the offsite work this agency is producing for you.

You start ranking for irrelevant keywords. You should already know the keywords you want to target, and your Google analytics can show you what key words are generating you traffic. If your keywords change drastically then be careful! If you're generating traffic from wrong terms then it's because you have had work targeting wrong keywords to your site.

There are many more ways to spot scam SEO agencies, but these are the most obvious. Be sure you do your homework, and if all else fails, just look for reviews.

Most Common SEO Scams:

There are many scams plaguing the SEO industry that result in a lot of websites being penalised and removed from the Search Engines Indexes. You have to bear in mind, the internet is a universe in itself, ever expanding and always evolving. In some instances it's always worth knowing about some of the more common scams in order to best avoid them in order to protect yourself from SEO scammers.

There is a scam that involves *"shadow domains"* which is where domains steer users to a site by using redirects in a deceptive manner. These are typically owned by a Search Engine Marketer who is claiming to work on their client's behalf. It may not always be the case that they stay working with this particular site so they may point this domain to a different site, most typically a competitor's domain. If this happens, it essentially means that this business/individual has paid for the competing site which usually ends up being owned by the search marketer they were working with.

There is also what's known as *"doorway pages"* which is another scam process. This is where pages loaded with keywords are inserted on the website – usually quite deep and hidden. What's usually apparent within these scams is that these pages usually contain links to the other clients of this search marketer and your site is being used as nothing more than a link farm.

What to look out for:

Unsolicited emails. These usually include phrases such as *"you're not on the search engines"* or *"we guarantee number 1 results on Google"* or *"we'll link with you on our website"*. If you receive any enquiries like this – ignore them. These are sent from spam agencies and companies that aren't looking to optimise you successfully nor are they looking to provide you with any substantial SEO advice.

Be sure to look into the market as well. If someone says they work for a particular agency – be sure to find reviews on them. If you're presented with a great deal of negative reviews or bad publicity then its worthwhile steering clear.

Also avoid companies that will call you from other countries. There are many companies that aim to link farm all over the world, and if you are being approached form an international SEO agency then it is more likely than not that they are looking to source your site for a link farm. Google want to see your site linking to local and national sites not sites from another country. What purpose would that achieve?

How to be sure your SEO agency is helping you

There are some fantastic SEO agencies out there, and provided you know what you're looking for they shouldn't be too hard to spot. Of course you'll need to assess a few things to be sure they are a good agency and that they won't cause your website any harm.

If an SEO agency can offer you any of the following you know you're on to a winner:

- Deliverables.
- Recommendations for improvement.
- Improved rankings.
- Your traffic goes down but your conversion rate and revenue go up.

Deliverables.

A decent SEO agency will show you what they are doing for you. They may not be able to show you first page results in all instances, but they will be able to provide you with evidence of things that they have done. They should be able to show you actual sites that link back to your own with dofollow links. They without question should be able to provide you with a site audit that includes what to do next.

They may even be able to provide you with new content for your site or changes on what is currently there, or at the very least recommendations. Most importantly they should provide you with reports. These could be weekly, monthly or quarterly to show you the work they have done and the effect(s) that work has had on your site. So long as they show you what they are doing and how they are doing it you have nothing to worry about.

Recommendations for improvement.

No SEO agency can help you optimise your site unless you help them. If they recommend you make certain changes or implementations then this should tell you that they want to work with you as a partner not for you. Be sure to help them with as much as they ask for as this will help them to generate the best possible results for you. Don't be alarmed if they ask you to set up social profiles on various social networks as this will help your SEO campaign, they will then make sure you integrate them with your homepage. In some cases they may ask you for a content marketing plan or to start a blog. They may request you add more content to your home page and optimise all content on your site.

This isn't an up sell or scam tactic offered by agencies, it serves a legitimate purpose for you to work together to generate the best results possible for your site.

Your ranking improves.

If you're agency is improving your rankings then you are in good hands. So long as you are ranking for your targeted keywords, you're on the first page of Google and you are also ranking for a variety of long tail keywords you know you're working with a reputable agency.

Your traffic goes down but your conversions and revenue go up!

Nobody wants to see the traffic to their site go down, but any decent SEO agency will reduce the amount of erroneous traffic you get to your site. With this in mind it usually means that you'll see greater conversions and revenue from this traffic as it is more relevant to your site and what you are looking to achieve.

This traffic will come from the right set of long tail keywords you optimise around and they will in turn be the right audience. If for instance you had black leather weatherproof boots you would see a higher conversion and revenue rate from the long tail key phrase "*black leather weatherproof boots*" than you would from a more generic less specific key phrases such as "*black boots*".

These points aren't as obvious as you might thing when it comes down to spotting some poor SEO agencies. Of course, without being an expert in SEO it's hard to establish who is or isn't going to be of benefit to your business. There are many things you can do to check the SEO agency you are in talks with.

Your checklist when finding the right SEO agency.

1. **Patience.** SEO takes time, so you'll need to wait a while before you see any hard hitting results. This can take a few months, but so long as they are keeping you in the loop with what they are doing, then you're on the right track.

2. **Do the research! Learn what you can about SEO.** Do your own research. There are many places out there where you can do your own SEO research Guides from companies such as quicksprout or perhaps the beginners guide to SEO from MOZ will help you to gain a firmer understanding of the SEO industry and what questions you should be asking.

3. **Be sure to work with your SEO agency.** Search engine optimisation is a team sport. You will need to become partners in order to ensure the best possible results by working together. If they're a

reputably agency and they ask you to do something to benefit your SEO campaign, help them out. Don't be afraid if they ask you to do things on a regular basis, as you'll need to put effort in on your side just as they will on theirs. Don't worry though they will let you know why they're asking for you to do it.

4. **Watch out for "*100% money back guarantee*" companies.** SEO is not an exact science. It never has been and it never will be. This is because Google are constantly releasing algorithmic and update changes that effect ranking positions. Any decent SEO agency can't guarantee their work. As they have to keep up with the industry changes, they can only do their best bearing in mind the search engines work is out of their control. This stands true for any agency that is guaranteeing you certain Search Engine Ranking Positions. These companies are to be avoided as you can't establish how many websites will be optimising for the same terms, how many of them have a larger SEO budget than you, and how many of them will brutally attack their competitors in search fields.

5. **Have a clear understanding.** This means you have to be sure to know what to expect from any SEO agency. You need to ensure that they are creating content and backlinks whilst also auditing the content and backlinks. Ensure they are able to provide you with a link profile whilst optimising conversion elements to your site. They should also be optimising you for local SEO and creating (where needed) social network profiles. All of these will have a great impact on your ranking ability.

6. **Keep tabs on them.** This may sound very paranoid, but you need to be sure you monitor them as you would any other form of marketing agency. Be sure to ask them what they are doing and how they are doing it. Don't be afraid to ask them for reports and be sure to read the reports that they send you.

To conclude, you have to be very aware of the implications SEO can have on your online business. You will either succeed or you will fail miserably. This marketing strategy is far too imperative to hand over to anyone on just a whim. You need to be sure you are as invested in the SEO process as this is without fail the most important marketing strategy you can implement. Think of it this way; SEO puts you in front of the customers that are looking for you and your products/services but just haven't found you yet.

Getting yourself started with SEO.

Don't be daunted by the number of steps there are to SEO. It is a very complicated process that doesn't generate results overnight. You need to ensure you have as many of the starting steps covered as possible prior to implementing an SEO campaign. Here are some key steps to follow to help cover your bases when it comes to optimising for your keywords successfully.

Keywords and concepts:

Always bear in mind, you are an expert in your industry, SEO agencies are experts in theirs. You should therefore start to establish what behaviours you want to be a part of and what terms you want to be associated with.

Be sure they are relevant. By doing this, ensure you are targeting the right people, writing the right content and being part of the conversations you want to be recognised for. You can do this by searching forums or social platforms to see what people are talking about and what keywords would be best to rank for.

Plan your content marketing.

By now you should have a firm idea of what keywords you would like to rank for. This means you should now be able to ensure you are able to put high quality relevant content on your website. You can do this by putting together an editorial plan by assessing what content is required to each area of your business that you are looking to target. The more concepts you target the more variations you can have of content creation. It's the best possible practice.

Be sure to check your site

In order to rank successfully within the search engines, you have to ensure you are indexing and creating content that can be seen and above all else is unique. You also need to make sure your code is search engine friendly.

This sounds harder than it is. Modern CMS systems provide search engine friendly code, and if you are using the platform WordPress then you are at an advantage as there are some reliable SEO plugins available. Of course these don't provide extensive SEO work to your site, but they can help ensure everything behind your site with reference to the technical SEO elements are in working order saving you time and money.

It's imperative you have a sitemap also. You need to be sure your users and the search engine spiders can accurately find their way around your site.

Don't underestimate your Metadata.

Metadata runs further than you may think. Content, images, PDF files and videos and social profiles are just some of the things than can contribute to Metadata on your site. Don't be daunted by this as this will be a huge advantage to your onsite optimisation strategies. You can be sure these files, images and content all target the phrases you are looking to rank for, whilst also ensuring your Meta titles and descriptions focus on some of the terms as well.

Social Importance.

Be sure to be active on social platforms. The key platforms are Facebook, Google+ and Twitter. You will develop a greater authority behind yourself if you have social profiles at the ready. This does not mean that you have to contract all of your employees into representing you through social channels, but it can certainly help. There are many ways in which social visibility can impact your search engine ranking positions.

Be sure you have an SEO expert.

Be it an agency or an employed individual, you need to ensure SEO remains a top priority for your marketing strategies. Just because someone is a write or a developer or indeed an analytical individual, does not mean that they have a full grasp of the SEO industry. You need to ensure you have a set person or company accountable for your online visibility as it will take up too much of your time to focus on daily. You need to ensure someone can cover this on a full time basis or at the very least a part time basis.

How Search Engines Operate:

Search Engines have many functions. They crawl, they index, they calculate and they serve. If you're not sure about what each of these processes involve then read on to find out more about each.

Crawling and Indexing

Search engines crawl and index each and every page on the internet. They crawl and index using links as these are paths that connect virtually all websites across the web.

This structure serves to link all pages in existence (from the search engines point of view). Search engines have automated robots called spiders or crawlers that through this link structure can reach billions upon billions of these interconnected documents. Once these pages/documents are found by the search engines, they then assess the code on them and pick up on and document selected pieces of these pages/files on their own hard drives in order to be recalled with a relevant query. In order for search engines to achieve this documentation and storage, they have data centres in cities all over the world to ensure maximum storage capacity as the internet is ever growing.

These facilities hold many thousands of machines processing vast amounts of information. Bear in mind, when a person performs a search on any major search engine, they expect results instantaneously, and even so much as a four second delay can cause them to use a search engine elsewhere. If you make a search on Google, you'll notice that prior to the listed results, it will tell you how many results were found in how many seconds.

How the Search Engines provide the answers to your queries.

When you search for something the search engines filter through all of their stored sites to provide you with a couple of things. Firstly they return only the results that are relevant to your search and they rank those results in order of importance or relevance to your search term.

However, the search engines step it up in this instance. They provide you with results that are relevant in more than just having a page with the words on it that you searched for. In the start-up of search engines they did exactly that, provide you with sites that had the phrase(s) listed on them that you were searching for. As a result they could see that these results weren't as useful as they had anticipated, so they went the extra mile. Nowadays, hundreds of factors are attributed to relevance.

Importance is very tough to quantify and search engines do their best to get it right. At present, importance is perceived by popularity. The greater a site/page/documents popularity, the more relevant the information within it must therefore be. Think about it this way, the more word of mouth you have recommending you online – the more relevant your services must be to the intended searchers. This process has been of great success to search engines and as a result they have continued to increase searcher's satisfaction by using these popularity metrics.

These factors aren't determined manually, instead the search engines create algorithms and processes that sort the relevant from the not so relevant to rank in order of relevance. These ranking factors are very extensive, so you can rest assured in the knowledge that these factors are set out to help searchers and those sites/pages/files hoping to be found. It is without question that you would rather be found for something relevant than not.

This may seem daunting and almost impossible to rank for, but provided you know what you are doing and indeed how to do it, you can use these factors and guidelines to rank accordingly.

How the search engines help you with their listed guidelines is not as daunting. Here is some simple SEO advice that will help you better understand each of the Search Engines.

Yahoo have outlined that there are several factors that will impact your search engine ranking positions such as:

- The number of sites linking to yours
- The content within your pages
- The discovery of additional sites
- Changes to their search algorithm.

Bing has their own outlines that they recommend.

- To ensure queries users may search for are visible within your page text
- To ensure all pages are limited to a certain size and topic. Usually one topic per page with a size no larger than 150KB.
- Ensuring every page has at least one static text link.
- And to ensure text that you want to be indexed is not present in images.

Google also provide guidelines for rankings as set out by their webmasters:

- They want you to make your pages for your users not for the search engines. They want you to avoid cloaking (presenting different content to search engines than you display to users) as ultimately Google look for customer satisfaction when ranking.
- Hierarchy your site. Do this by attributing links to your site and ensuring every page should have at least one static text link.
- Be sure your site is useful and information rich. Make sure your pages clearly and accurately describe your attributed content.
- Keep your <title> and ALT attributes descriptive but most importantly accurate.
- Keep any links you have on any given page at a reasonable number. These can be anywhere between 1 and 100 (depending on the size of the page) but never more than 100.

Don't be put off by these extensive methodologies. Through methods such as patent analysis, live testing and experiments, Search Engine Marketers are able to understand how these operations work and ultimate how to use these guidelines to their own/their client's advantage by adhering to all set procedures to rank well.

How users interact with the search engines

In order for any website to rank well on Search Engines, you have to understand your target demographic. You have to be able to understand how your audience searches and more to the point, how they use search so you can reach theme effectively. Here is how you can do it step by step:

- Experience your market's need for an answer/solution or simply just a piece of information.

- Calculate their need in set phrases and queries.

- Search for that query.

- Click on any given result that you are presented with.

- See if that site is of relevance or an answer to the given query.

- If it's not relevant go back and click on links to find it any of the sites listed are relevant.

- If you can't find anything of relevance to that search term – try using another query.

You don't need to execute these studies in order to establish several things. The search market is very popular and it reaches billions of people across the globe. More than this, the first half of results within page one are critical to online visibility.

Not many users venture onto page two or beyond. First position rankings obviously provide the largest amount of traffic, but it also provides trust to your consumers and importance within your market. It's also imperative to state that a huge amount of offline economic activity starts with searches on the internet.

If you are looking for something on a search engine, you want relevance, you want reliability and you also want them to be recommended. This is what the search engines are looking to provide you with. Ultimately they are a business and they want you to come back, so the information they aim to provide you has to be relevant to what you are looking for, otherwise you would use another search engine, and they don't want that.

They want you to keep coming back, which is why they are constantly changing their outlines and methods when it comes to rankings, in order to provide you (their user) with the best results possible so you keep going back.

Search Engine friendly design and development: the basics

As extensive as Search Engine crawling tactics may be, they are limited with how they can crawl and interpret content in order to display the best results. They require both on page and off page optimisation in order to rank more effectively.

What you'll need to help the bots crawl and index your site more sufficiently:

- **Index your content.**
  You need to ensure your content and the visible material on your website is in HTML text format. If your images, videos and files are not in text HTML format, then they will be invisible to the search engines which will impact you as these files will be relevant to what you are offering.

  Think of it this way, if you were to be using a very out dated browser and your images wouldn't load – would you rather see a big empty box with a cross in it, or a box with text describing the image you should see?
   You can do this by placing these files on your page in the HTML text on the page. However, there are more options available. With images in a .gif, .jpg or .png format, you can assign them "ALT attributes" in HTML, meaning you can provide a text version of your visual content in this process. Video and audio content should come with an accompanying transcript so that the search engines can index them.

- **Ensure your Link Structures can be crawled.**
  Search engines require content in order to rank,
  however they also need websites to have link
  structures that they can crawl. If you hide or
  obfuscate your navigation then the simple fact is
  the search engines won't be able to rank you.

  Unless you provide direct crawlable links that point
  to all of your pages, the search engines will not be
  able to rank them. When the search bots index
  your site – with the pages they can't access they
  don't exist. Regardless of the content, the
  keywords and the marketing you have put into
  these pages, if they aren't accessible, they aren't
  going to be ranked.

- **Keyword targeting and Usage**
  Keywords are the stepping stones of search. The
  entire search marketing process is based on
  keywords. As your site is crawled and indexed, it is
  documented in the search engines attributed
  keyword sections in order to be readily accessible
  for a search of that kind. Essentially any term you
  wish for your site to be indexed under, you have to
  ensure that keyword is part of the indexable
  content within your site.

These three steps are imperative to any SEO advice you
will find. Of course, the whole concept is much deeper
and greater than content and links, but fundamentally this
is where you can make the bulk of your impact within the
search market. These are of course useless without all of
the other SEO boxes ticked, but provided you can get
your head around these, then there is no reason you

wouldn't be able to extend your search engine marketing knowledge further.

Keyword Research

Without a doubt keyword research is fundamental to any Search Marketing campaign you could implement. It cannot be overstated how imperative this is to your online marketing strategies. You need to be able to understand your market extensively and come to terms with what they are searching for. What you may think is entirely relevant to target may not be as your market may be looking for something else. It's very much down to semantics.

Every phrase or word that is typed into a search engine is recorded. To better understand the value of a particular keyword, you need to assess several things. One, how many people are searching for that term. Two, the competition levels associated to that term. Three, your chances of ranking for that term, and four your chances of converting for that term.

To put it another way, if you know that the term "*shoes*" (as an example) generates 165,000 searches a month, and it's very competitive, are you going to realistically be able to rank on the first page? Probably not – however, the term is also very generic and may not have a high conversion rate with it either. If you were to aim to target something more relevant in which case such as "*men's shoes*" which has 40,500 searches a month, your chances of ranking on the first page are that much higher, but although there may not be as high a traffic volume the conversion rate will be higher as the searchers have specified what shoes they are looking for.

This brings us on to the understanding of long tail keywords. Long tail keywords are phrases that are more specific and indeed longer than generic terms. If you take the example of "shoes" from above, this term is very generic and not overly specific. If you were to take another more specific example such as *"men's smart brogue shoes"* this is a long tail keyword.

The benefit of targeting longer tail keywords is that they are more specific which will ultimately lead to a higher conversion rate as the searcher has done the hard work of specifying what they are looking for. The competition attributed to these key words is minimal in comparison to the more generic terms, but the bounce rate will undoubtedly be lower and the conversion rate higher. To put it in business terms – would you rather be put in front of 100,000 where 0.0001% (10) visitors convert; or a term that generates 10,000 where 1% (100) or visitors convert?

In order to best assess this, you need a firm grasp on the insight of keyword difficulty. To do this, you need to understand the demand for the terms you are looking to optimise around, but ultimately the work required to optimise for these words/phrases. If the competition is already very high and the results on the first page are fighting against each other for the top spots, then realistically this is probably not a term you can target if you are a start-up, unless you are willing to wait years to notice any kind of results. Start with the easier terms to then eventually move on to the more difficult key phrases and words.

Showing how content, usability and user experience affect SERPs

It's all well and good providing the Search Engines results based on relevance but it doesn't just boil down to key words. The major search engines always set out to provide the best results for users. This means that in order to rank well sites have to be easy to use for the user – meaning they not only have to be clear and concise in the content they provide, but also that they are easy to navigate and to understand.

It is fundamental to understand that these elements go hand in hand. These sites must provide clear directions and information relevant to the query at hand. If you are an ecommerce site for instance, it must be clear on how to add an item to a basket and how to move from the basket to the checkout. More than this, the sites have to be compatible with all browsers and devices whilst also looking professional. Finally, they must also deliver high quality, credible, legitimate content to the user.

Search engines may be able to assess content such as text, images and videos, but fundamentally they can't understand they content in the way a human user can. So if they aren't able to comprehend the validity of the semantics on the page, then how do they accurately assess the usability of the page? They do this by assessing link profiles and layouts of sites. So through sitemaps and online visibility they are able to assess which sites have more authority and which have a greater popularity behind them. From this information you will then see how this process affects the rankings.

As a user you will appreciate a site that is clear and concise and can take you from point A to point B clearly and easily. If you were to search for a term of any kind and you were presented with two results – one being a text heavy essay layout site with a white background and black text with no images, no menu or no pictures and the other being a clearly laid out site with colour schemes, relevant attributed images, a clear menu and clear calls to action – it goes without saying which one you would trust more.

Your site will rank better if you are writing it for your users and their experience rather than for the search engines themselves. They may not be able to tell the difference directly, but based on points of recommendation, back link profiles and concrete text layouts, then they will be able to assess which sites the market prefers.

Fundamentally if your business is based entirely or partially online, you need to ensure you get it right. Give your users a reason to come back. Make sure you give them a reason to recommend you to other users and fundamentally make sure you are able to interest them. This may sound rather difficult, but view it from your own perspective. Think of the websites that you like and establish why you like them. Look into their layout, their sitemaps and their content to best realise why you keep going back to them.

In conclusion, all websites are different, but providing they serve their purpose accurately and they entice their users to come back then they are doing it right.

How to grow your online popularity and link profile

When search engines crawl the web they are looking to travel the web through links like we would use roads. Think of link profiles as maps for the search bots. More than this they are words of mouth or votes to a particular website hence the attributed authority.

Thanks to this methodology, growing the link profile of a website is now imperative in gaining attention and traffic. So you need to know how to work at this effectively.

Building links is very much an art, and it is extremely challenging for any Search Engine Optimisation marketer. It is however critical in achieving long term success. It's worth hiring an SEO agency to provide a robust backlink profile to your website as this will provide a huge advantage to your site and it will significantly raise the bar for your competitors when attempting to rank against you.

Where to start:

Link Signals and what to look out for: Prior to implementing a link building strategy there are several things you need to know, with particular reference to the elements of a link and how this is used by the search engine and how they factor into the rating of the links in algorithms.

- **Global popularity:**
  The more popular a site is, the more links from that site will matter. Ensuring local, topic-specific links is a good start but you'll need some powerful link partners to hit the top spots.

- **Local popularity:**
  This is where links from specific sites within a local community matter more than links you can get from

general sites. Think of it this way, if you're a Manchester based company and nobody in Manchester can recommend you, you don't stand much of a chance of hitting the national market.

- **Anchor Text:**
Undisputedly of the strongest factors search engines use when ranking sites. If you have many links pointing to a page with the right keywords then you'll have a very good chance of ranking well for that particular key phrase.

- **Trust Rank**:
a lot of websites out there are spam. Search engines filter out the spam by measuring the trust of sites based on link graphs. Earning links from highly trusted domains leads to a greater boost within the ranking system.

- **Link neighbours:**
Be sure to be wise to link to sites carefully and don't be afraid to be selective. If it looks like spam it probably is so best to try and avoid it.

- **Editorial accumulation:**
These are links that are accumulated naturally and these are obtained by pages that want to reference your content or your business. The only work you need to worry about creating here is citation material.

- **Approval and suggestions:**
Whether you're looking into bloggers, directories or paid links you have to be sure that they create a value to your site, through filling out forms. Be wary of paid links though as these are very risky to

implement and you can be penalised for going overboard.

- **Self-created:**
  Many websites offer the chance to create links through guest books, blog comments, user profiles or forum signatures. These are low in value, but can have an impact on your ranking. Be careful not to use automated methods of this kind of link generation as this is spam and you won't do well out of it.

So how do you go about implementing the best possible link strategy?

- **Page ranking for relevant search terms:**
  Sounds obvious but ultimately the best way to determine how well a search engine values your page is to search for the terms you are already trying to target (try searching for you title tag and headline). Pages that rank well will be more valuable than those that don't.

- **Google page rank:**
  Pages with high page rank seemingly tend to pass on more like value than those with little or none.

- **Google Blog search:**
  this is the only tool online provided by Google that offers accurate back link information. Although this may only show links from blogs, there is still a great value ins seeing what pages have authority in the blogosphere as this can help indicate if the value of a link will pass.

It will take time and experience to become comfortable in these areas as they involve search engine traffic.

Through using your own analytics you should be able to accurately determine whether your SEO campaign is successful.

Increases in traffic followed by regular crawling and more referring links typically indicate a well-managed campaign. It's worth noting that if you see traffic rising from Bing and Yahoo while it's not rising in Google, this may suggest you need more authoritative and trustworthy links in order to see a rise in your SERPs on Google.

Search Engine Misconceptions

There are many misconceptions attributed to the Search Market Industry, which is undisputedly one of the biggest reasons it has been given such a bad reputation.

There are many organisations out there that claim to be the best or the cheapest that only offer you the chance to spend your money and generate less traffic and lose out on essential traffic.

We all know someone that's been burnt by a dodgy SEO agency, and we all don't want to be in their shoes. Perfectly understandable. Let's run through a few so you are aware of a scam if you see one.

- **Search engine submission:**
  Back in the 90s you had to submit your website to the search engines in order to be ranked on them. After this submission a bot would then crawl the site and store it accordingly. This process did not last long. All submissions now are automatic and providing you have a link profile behind yourself there is no reason you won't be indexed. Nowadays search engine submission is useless as well as 14 years out of date. If someone offers you a search engine submission – they need reeling into the 21st century. They clearly don't know what they are talking about – so don't give them the satisfaction.

- **Meta Tags:**
  It used to be that Meta Tags were by in large virtually solely responsible for ranking. This is no longer the case as people spammed this process beyond belief. They can help count for part of your

overall SEO strategy but overall, they don't hold much weight.

- **Keyword stuffing:**
A lot of SEO "experts" will claim that there is an equation you need to follow when writing content that divides the number of words on a page by the number of times a keyword is mention and based on the answer determines   your ranking position. This isn't the case. Use keywords intelligently and logistically. Not every other word and not extensively. Keep it natural.

- **Paid Search helps boost organic results:**
This is a theory that a lot of people think is true. By upping your PPC expenditure you will improve your organic rankings. This has never been proven nor has it ever been an explanation to SERPs. So long as the existing differences between these two metrics stay apparent, it will never be that Paid helps to benefit organic. This is entirely fictional.

- **Personalisation:**
Many people believe personalisation of sites can help boost rankings. It's shown that more than 90% of queries were unaffected by personalisation tactics, and whilst rankings and their changes can be dramatic, this only happens when there is a substantial query volume from a specific user around a specific topic.

Be sure you know your myths from your facts when implementing your SEO strategy. SEO advice that matters.

How to measure and track your success

Anything you can measure can undisputedly be improved upon. If you can measure your activity and success on Search Engine Optimisation you can indeed improve on it. You can track data regarding your rankings, referrals, backlink profiles and social activity.

You can check your statistics through your Google analytics and here you will be able to look into how much of your traffic is being generated through Search Engine Optimisation. This is usually labelled as Organic traffic. It is imperative to keep track of your visits every month so you can assess the best marketing strategies behind your site.

 Your Google analytics will tell you what keywords you are being found for on search engines, what referral traffic you are generating and how many visitors are coming through to your site from.

On top of this you can also use other metrics to help assess your traffic and your market. Here are some following tools you may find handy:

- Yahoo Site query: - this will redirect you to Yahoo's site explorer and you can see how many pages and lists yahoo has on a site in their index.

- Yahoo Link and link domain queries: this is very reliable. This tool helps show link profiles of particular domains and Yahoo also include nofollow links to give you a better idea as to what sites have what link profile behind them.

- Bing offer the same services with the additional IP query. This will show the pages that Microsoft has found on the given IP address. This can be particularly useful in identifying shared hosting and seeing other sites attributed to that particular IP.

When seeking the best possible SEO advice, be sure to do your own research. Don't get involved in the SEO industry blind as it won't work in your favour. Be sure you do your research and homework to be confident with any SEO agency or person you may hire to help you rank on the major search engines for your relevant key terms.

Google's Pigeon Update and what you need to know

Sharing yet another animal comparison, the pigeon update has brought some serious rocking to the SEO market. For a long time SEO agencies and experts have always advised starting on a local SEO coverage and then focusing on national and international terms where applicable. The pigeon update however seems to be giving local directory sites better visibility. This had been previous referred to as Google's "*Yelp Problem*".

What you may not know is earlier in the year (2014) Yelp had accused the Search Engine Giant of manipulating their results to show Google's own local listings and content way above any directory pages. Yelp claimed that this was even the case when users specifically searched for terms including "yelp" in the phrases.

Since this report was made, Google have now addressed and responded to this issue. So for lack of a better phrase you could say that this problem has now been addressed.

But it isn't just the directory Yelp that has been affected by this update. Other local directories have been boosted as a result to the point of less well known directories being area specific. So provided you are searching for local terms such as "*Salon Liverpool*" you should see the results speak for themselves.

However, this update has had an impact   on local businesses as well as directories. Search and phrase dependant of course, you should now start to see individual businesses in the top organic rankings, provided there is no directory listing for that term.

Depending on how generic a term is will depend on how many directory listings you get for that term. For instance generic terms such as *"Restaurants London"* will warrant multiple directory listings however something more specific such as *"Pizzeria Bristol"* will deliver more individual business website rankings.

Essentially this means that directories and directory style sites are now achieving higher visibility on Search Engine Ranking Positions since the release of the Pigeon update. Since the release of Pigeon Google have stated that *"this update ties local results more closely to standard web ranking signals"*. What this also means is that smaller local businesses are now going to have to work a lot harder to optimise for local terms on a generic platform as directories now dominate these platforms.

Although the Pigeon algorithm may be a saving grace for directories, it's going to be a long hard road for independent local businesses. There will no doubt be ways to overcome this challenge put in place in due course, but for the short term this will act as a massive blow to businesses that were generating (or at least were hoping to generate) a lot of business through organic search traffic.

Google's Panda Update – the basics

Panda was released in early 2011 and a lot of websites were hit as a result of this. This update affected a massive 11% of search queries. This may not sound like a huge amount, but at the time of this update there were an average 4,717,000,000 searches on Google every day. This means that a whopping 51,887,000 search queries a day were impacted as a result of the Panda update.

The intention of this update was to lower the ranking of "low quality" sites and ultimately deliver better results for high quality sites. As a result of the Panda update, Google released a blog on what you need in order to be recognised as a high quality site.

Panda boils down to the content on a site. For years many marketers were trying to work their way around the Search Engines by filling their sites with unnatural copy to try and rank well for their targeted keywords. More than this some websites were entirely duplicating other websites content in order to rank well for specific key terms.

 This led to Google implementing an "*over-optimisation penalty*". What this means, is that Google were recognising that poor quality content (and indeed duplicated content) were impacting the search market by ranking well for particular terms essentially effecting high quality sites for achieving great search results online. As a result, Google stated that such pages should be blocked from being indexed and ultimately removed from the search query results if they were not re-written. Be warned however, that rewriting content you have/had been penalised for may not be enough to get the penalty lifted.

What you should know: Panda was put in place to stop spammy sites from ranking well for terms that high quality hard working sites deserved. This means that so long as you are natural and high quality you will rank well. If you try to manipulate the system and cheat keyword targeting and spam then you're not going do very well in the search market.

Keep your content and info unique and natural. Don't try to manipulate the Search Engines as your audience will pick up on this and chances are – if they see spam – they're not going to come back.

How Penguin defeated Black Hat SEO

When most people think of penguins, they think of the cute little birds that walk (or waddle) upright that you can find in the southern hemisphere or at the zoo. Or you may think of the publishing company that offer great quality literature. Or for the fashion folk out there you may think of the clothing brand. For the Search Engine Optimisation Community Penguin was a saving grace to al white hat SEO tactics that were being largely undermined by black-hat tactics.

This update first hit the search community in April 2012. Its aim was to obliterate rankings for websites that were violating the Google Webmaster Guideline's on how to rank well by implementing unnatural strategies (that the industry calls black-hat) such as link farming, repetition of content and spamming.

These sites were getting to the top spots quick by trying to manipulate Google's indexing by making them think they had lots of links and content attributed to their site (which they did) but it was not of a high quality ultimately affecting those that had high quality white hat work behind their sites.

Penguin is similar to the Panda update as both aim to provide the best possible experience for users and get rid of those websites that don't.

With each new release of the Penguin update a percentage of queries have been affected. When it was first released (April 2012) the update impacted around 3% (154,020,000) searches a day. Their second release (May 2012) impacted 0.1% (5,134,000) searches a day. Their third update (October 2012) impacted around 0.3% (15,402,000) searches a day. Then when Penguin 2.0

was released (may 2013) it impacted 2% (118,440,000) of queries a day.

It's quite clear that each release of Penguin has significantly impacted the Search market, and it's also clear to see how many sites were violating the Google Webmaster guidelines for ranking.

Ensure that any SEO work you implement to your website is natural, and doesn't violate any of the guidelines and procedures put in place by Google otherwise you will be penalised as a result, and this will dramatically affect your online traffic from search and attributed conversion rates.

Google's hummingbird and implications

Hummingbird is yet another algorithm implemented by Google to help provide higher quality SERPs. Released in August 2013, this update was very much all about the semantics.

Hummingbird is the update that reads text as a whole and deciphers synonyms within the content and the context in which it was written. By this, simply think of a query you might make on Google, and due to the hummingbird algorithm, Google is able to determine the intention of your search to therefore provide you with the most relevant results. This is very intricate, and it was a long time coming.

From hummingbird now, each word within a query is taken into consideration to best evaluate the meaning of the query. For content marketer's, this is a whole new story as now you not only have to take into consideration the terms users may be searching for, but you also have to be aware of why they may be searching for that product/service in the first place. This way you can better target your content to answer their query rather than just repeat the keywords they have searched for.

Hummingbird is an update like no other, as it doesn't have a strict protocol or procedures to follow. With other updates – they have a check list to adhere to – but hummingbird almost has a mind of its own. When users search in natural language (it's alarming how many searchers don't), hummingbird takes the natural language, and the semantics behind the search to generate the best possible results. The intent of hummingbird is to match the search with sites/pages that provide a matching meaning to the search query rather than just the words alone.

This means that with any content you now provide on your site you no longer have to worry about including all of your keywords. Instead of including *"business location"* as a pair as searchers use this term quite frequently, you can now be more natural by talking about your *"business"* and later or earlier mentioning the *"location"*.

Hummingbird is without doubt the most thought provoking update Google has implemented and it certainly now means the Search Engine Optimisation industry has a greater creative licence with regards to content as they are now able to be as natural as possible, which in turn should provide sites and pages with a higher user experience (and hopefully conversion rate) as the more relevant your page the higher your rankings to their queries, making it easier than ever to target your demographic through search.

Keywords and their attributed variations

Keywords are critical to research in order to rank for the most relevant and searched for terms to your business. It's worth understanding that keyword research is essential and not all people search for the same phrases even though they may want the same products and/or services.

This is where keyword variations come into account. Google appreciated this factor and released a matching behaviour for phrases and keywords. This is where phrases and exact match keywords would automatically be partnered with misspellings, abbreviations and the like for these terms. Google released an example saying if you only had *"the exact match keyword"* such as *"white tennis shoes"* in your ad group, then instead of generating results for that one query, this term would now generate rankings for an alternative version of that phrase such as *"white tennis shoe"* or misspelled queries such as *"wite tennis shoes"*.

This change was significant to Search Engine Optimisation considering close to 10% of queries made are misspelled. Matching behaviour is largely attributed to PPC and AdWords behaviours in these instances which is where you can enable your *"include close variations"* option in your AdWords campaign. This helps to ensure you generate as much relevant traffic as possible without having to include every possible relevant term into your campaign.

As of September 2014 Google will no longer make it optional to opt out of close variant matching. Meaning you'll see a 7% increase in traffic, but you'll also see a 7% increase in expenditure.

This information is all well and good, but what does this mean for SEO? Well, if you have an SEO campaign where you are focusing on *"Key word 1" "Key phrase 2"* and *"Search term 3"* you need to make your content more natural so as to be picked up for additional variations and misspellings. Fortunately this doesn't mean you have to include every possible misspelling nor every possible variation of your keywords or phrases, but it can't hurt to look into the attributed variations associated with your key phrases to include them on the odd occasion to give you more authority.

If you're already working with an SEO agency – they should have already advised you on this process. If not – then they're not doing a very good job for you. Through targeting a set of varying keywords all around the same topic, you can generate the most amount of traffic. For example:

Term:	Monthly Searches:
Keyword	**1,000**
Keyword 1	750
Keyword 2	500
Keyword 3	250
Key phrase	**1,000**
Key phrase 1	750
Key phrase 2	500
Key phrase 3	250

Where you may have only been focusing on *"keyword"* and *"key phrase"* previously, you're only looking to generate a total of 2,000 searches a month to your site. By including the variations attributed to *"Keyword"* and *"Key phrase"*, you'd be able to generate an addition 3,000 searches a month. That means that you'd be able to more than double your potential traffic exposure by targeting the variations also.

With these variations you are also helping to generate greater authority for the main key term also, which will help to further boost your rankings. So instead of focusing on 10 different keywords, you should look to target 2 separate keywords with four variations of each. Start small and aim high.

This is imperative SEO advice and you should be aware of these factors before trying to rank blindly as the more info you have to rank the better your chances will be.

Google Analytics

Google analytics is one of the key tools you will need to implement in order to monitor your online success. You can get two versions of analytics, standard and premium. He standard campaign is free but the premium version comes with an annual charge of £90,000, it's pretty safe to assume you'd probably not be reading this if you could afford the yearly charge, so let's run through what you can get with Google analytics standard free version and how this can help you monitor your online progress.

Google analytics provide standard users with many things. Firstly you're probably going to want to be aware of the self-service support forum they have. You'll probably end up on this a few times in the initial set up of your analytics – but don't worry we've all been there.

You'll be limited on a couple of things, but if you're an SME or smaller corporate company – this shouldn't really matter too much. You will be limited to receiving info on 10 million hits, 50,000 rows of data, data refreshing every 24 hours and campaign management. You will also be able to integrate your AdWords campaign and generate multi-channel reporting.

However you will only be able to implement 5 custom variables which should suit, but the premium level only goes up to 50. But this shouldn't be too much of a worry as you'll also see great availability with segmentation, custom reporting, intelligence info, real time data, social reporting, mobile tracking and data export.

If you want to see how traffic is coming to your site, what it's doing when it's on your site, what your bounce rate is and equally what your conversion rate is, then you should implement Google analytics. GA can also help you assess your organic search performance and keyword targeting. So this is a really insightful little tool you should most certainly implement in order to best assess your website.

Without analytics you wouldn't be able to see how successful your online marketing efforts are, so it's a really crucial tool to help further your performance online.

It also breaks the information down into visual charts and graphs to help gain a better visual perspective of statistics and insights to your website without having to trawl through extensive tables and charts, although that option is available if you require it.

It's also imperative to know how to set up loyalty metrics within your Google Analytics account. Customer loyalty is by far one of the most substantially strong elements a business can implement. The beauty of GA is that it automatically collects data that can accurately provide you with loyalty metrics.

A lot of marketers use the column indicating returning visitors to suggest customer loyalty. In place of using the information and data Google Analytics provides, decide what metrics you want to analyse and how you can implement them in your Google Analytics account.

There is always a way to explore your customer loyalty, it just boils down to the type of insights you are looking to generate and ultimately how much time you have to generate them.

How Social Media can impact your SEO

Many people still don't see the value of Social Media when it comes to SEO. A few years ago, your thoughts would have been completely right. Nowadays – not so much, in fact, not at all.

It's great if your website is popular and has great content but this isn't enough to get you to the top spots on the search engines now. This is why you need social media to help you as a social media presence will help to further boost your SEO campaign. Gone are the days where only great content and inbound links affected your rankings.

When social media took off it changed the procedure of search engine optimisation, for the better! Social signals (in other word likes, retweets, +1s and so on) are now incorporated in search engine procedures to get you to the top spots. Again, this is very much like word of mouth and online votes proving your authority and reliability as a business online. This is a great way for search engines to measure the popularity of your site, and as standard the more popular and trusted, relevant and reliable your site is, the higher you will rank.

Social Media and Search Engine Optimisation very much go hand in hand. The two depend on each other in order to succeed. Brands are found predominantly through search and social. Visitors from organic search have the highest conversion rates, and social activity heightens brand awareness. Being two sides of the same coin they need each other to succeed. Through social you can reach your customers directly and through search you can generate new business. Moreover, you can distribute unique and relevant content through your social channels to further your SEO strategies.

What's more, you can encourage people to share your content through their own social channels which helps to connect your brand virally on the internet. This means anything you post on social channels has the potential of reaching hundreds or thousands of additional prospects. Ultimately you have to ensure your content will be read and shared by your followers. The point of social media is not just the likes but the sharing of the content. It is the literal online version of word of mouth, and this helps to generate new business.

In order to do this effectively, as a brand you have to stop talking about yourself and start talking about your customers. Encourage engagement and generate conversations with your target audience. Asking your customers to share your content is an effective way of helping gain visibility online and promote your content by reaching new audiences.

But why stop there? You should boost your images and your social profiles as this will further impact your Search Engine Optimisation. Images can have a big impact on SEO as these are visual pieces of content.

And Google+ is a whole different story. When you create a website you can assign authorship through your Google+ profile. This feature allows you to connect your Google+ profile directly to your website which in turn sees you as being more trusted which will help you to rank better.

But don't forget to measure your social performance! Your goals can be measured and by doing this you're assessing your efforts. Through utilising social presence you can generate leads, drive sales and increase your brand awareness. Be sure to focus on these metrics rather than likes as you could have 100,000 likes but nobody shares or follows you so they will be pretty useless.

What's even better is that you can measure traffic to your website from Social Media in your Google Analytics. This is a quick and simple process that gives you definitive figures of how many people came through to your site from social which helps you to assess what percentage of your overall website traffic was generated through social. See for yourself – it's worth having.

Can your domain impact your Search Engine Optimisation?

Let's start this off with understanding exactly what a domain is. Domains are the internet addresses for websites that are visible to people. Root domains are the hierarchy of domains and they can be bought from various entities (such as Go Daddy or 123 reg). Root domains are things such as example.com, eg.org, or forexample.co.uk. And then come subdomains. These are what are known as "third level" domains that are part of a larger domain such as blog.forexmaple.com (this being a subdomain of forexample.com).

It's good to know some points prior to purchasing a domain for your business. Hyphens are a no go for domains. Hyphens are seen as detracting the credibility of a site and often indicate a spam site. Try to avoid uncommon top-level domains (such as .cc.info etc.) as these often also indicate spam processes. Length is also an issue to watch out for. Try to avoid having a domain longer than 15 characters in length as the shorter the domain, the easier to remember.

Domains can affect your SEO. There are a few things you will need into consideration prior to purchasing a domain to ensure best practice for SEO.

- **Top Level Domains**
  In order to maximise direct traffic it is often recommended to purchase multiple top level domains such as example.com and example.co.uk but keep them to known Top Level Domains (TLDs) and not things such as .biz or .info as this is seen as low quality to search engines. You want to be seen as authoritative as possible and TLDs are the best way to achieve this.

- **Domain memory**.
  Being short and easy to remember helps to reinforce word of mouth advertising which can ultimately lead to more people searching for your company online. It's time consuming to type in a lengthy domain and there is a greater chance of spelling errors or typos if this is the case, so be sure your domain is memorable and simple.

- **Redirecting domains**
  Redirecting domains are often devalued by the search engines as they aren't functional websites in themselves so Google don't like to index them.

- **Subdomains**
  Subdomains use different metrics in the SEO industry so try to ensure your website has a subfolder instead such as example.com/blog

- **Keep them keyword rich.**
  You can benefit in a couple of ways by having a keyword rich domain. Domains are ranking factors, and if you already have the keywords in your domain you'll do even better when ranking. On top of this users will search for your domain name as well as your targeted keywords which help to give you more authority and branding. Be sure to keep it high quality though otherwise Google will negatively impact your site.

- **Avoid using hyphens.**
  If you have words in your domain that you want to separate you should avoid using hyphens as these are seen as spammy tactics. Try underscores or just combining the words.

Your domain will have an impact on your search engine performance so be sure everything to do with it looks natural and concise. Imagine you're a viewer to your site – and you see your URL. Be sure to check that you are completely happy with it before implementing it.

July 2014 and the changes Google implemented

July 2014 saw four things change with Google. These changes were around authorship, in-depth articles, video listings and Pigeon. All of these changes saw impacts in SERPs (Search Engine Ranking Positions) and these were a step above the ordinary organic and traditional changes Google has been known to make. Let's explore each of these in more detail:

Authorship:

Technically this happened at the end of June but the results were pretty clear by July. It all started with a Google employee (John Mueller) making a less than anticipated announcement on his Google+ profile. With 41,000 followers his post was seen very quickly and it rocked the Search Engine Optimisation field. He said *"We've been doing lots of work to clean up on the visual design of our search results, in particular creating a better mobile experience and a more consistent design across devices. As a part of this, we're simplifying the way authorship is shown in mobile and desktop search results, removing the profile photo and circle count."*

Authorship changes have been made in the past but this change really rocked the boat. The premise of authorship was to generate more traffic through trust metrics as people could see who had written the info and could connect with them through their social channel. No SEOs had foreseen this change. It didn't really make sense. Over the next few days' searches with author photos dropped from an average of 20% to an average of 0%. This had quite the impact.

The concept of authorship is still present and information about the author are still being shown, but the visual element of their picture and circle count now no longer exists.

In-depth articles:

In-depth articles don't really get much attention in the search demographic by SEO experts or searchers themselves; however they had slowly been gaining Search Engine Ranking Position shares. In July 2014 overnight, in-depth article presence saw an increase of 6.0% coverage to 12.7%. It's not entirely clear why this change was implemented and it can now be seen that more in-depth results are showing for competitive ranking terms.

Video listings:

When you search for certain content you have the option to search for video content. We've all used the videos tab, and sometimes you don't need to as they can be present in the organic web results. These videos came with thumbnail images. Note the past tense in that sentence.

This change seems to have played focus on the thumbnails of videos and it would seem Google don't deem the thumbnails to be overly important. With Google offering mega-video appearances on the search engines also this change hasn't been specified nor mentioned by Google. Yet another unexplainable change within the search engine industry.

Pigeon:

The Pigeon update hit the local Search Engine Ranking Positions hard. It has dramatically changed how Google determines a searcher's location. Google used to offer their own local search results that would give you a brief bit of information about local businesses followed by a rating (issued by users and reviews) and their contact information.

From this update local results (the local listings Google would categorise) fell by nearly 25%. Pigeon is a new update so Google will no doubt be implementing updates and tweaks over the coming months.

This Pigeon update has seemingly made is harder to rank for local terms (following the directory changes they implemented not long before) so it would seem that it is now harder than ever for local businesses to optimise around local terms. It's more likely that Google are trying to make it easier to rank for local terms, but the Pigeon update will need to be improved somewhat before that happens.

All these changes show how quickly Google can make changes and how dramatically this can affect search for both Search Engine Optimisers and indeed users.

Conclusion:

There are many factors that implement your chances of optimising well on the search engines. The simple fact is, Search Engine Optimisation is a highly competitive industry with more businesses than ever before looking to compete online in order to maximise their revenue, traffic, customer loyalty and brand awareness.

Understanding the different elements of SEO is imperative in order to implement an effective SEO strategy. There are onsite and offsite outlines in order to take on the search market. With Google averaging 4 billion searches a day (in other words 166.6 million searches an hour, 2.7 million searches a minute or 47,000 search queries a second); Google is certainly not short of users. Putting yourself in front of these users on this search engine simply means putting yourself in front of a larger, more reputable, but most importantly more relevant target market.

Google is the internet giant of search, so it is imperative to adhere to all of Google's guidelines and practices as otherwise you won't do very well. It's important to know the fact from the fluff within the industry, and hopefully there has been enough information here to conclude this.

References

1. Anderson, M. (2011). *How Google Panda & Places Updates Created A Rollercoaster Ride For IYP Traffic.* Available: http://searchengineland.com/how-google-panda-places-updates-created-a-rollercoaster-ride-for-iyp-traffic-101683. Last accessed Jan 2014.
2. Anon. (2003). *Spamdexing.* Available: http://www.wordspy.com/words/spamdexing.asp. Last accessed December 2013.
3. Anon. (2007). *New: Content analysis and Sitemap details, plus more languages.* Available: http://googlewebmastercentral.blogspot.co.uk/2007/12/new-content-analysis-and-sitemap.html. Last accessed Jan 2014.
4. Anon. (2010). *Search Engine Optimization Starter Guide.* Available: http://static.googleusercontent.com/media/www.google.co.uk/en/uk/webmasters/docs/search-engine-optimization-starter-guide.pdf. Last accessed Jan 2014.
5. Anon. (2012). *A Simple Step by Step Guide to SEO.* Available: https://blog.kissmetrics.com/simple-guide-to-seo/. Last accessed Jan 2014.
6. Anon. (2012). *Another step to reward high-quality sites.* Available: http://googlewebmastercentral.blogspot.co.uk/2012/04/another-step-to-reward-high-quality.html. Last accessed July 2014.
7. Anon. (2012). *New matching behaviour for phrase and exact match keywords.* Available: http://adwords.blogspot.co.uk/2012/04/new-

matching-behavior-for-phrase-and.html. Last accessed Jan 2014.

8. Anon. (2014). *7 Secrets To Keeping Your New Email Address Spam-Free.* Available: http://www.webspam.org/7-secrets-to-keeping-your-new-email-address-spam-free/. Last accessed Jan 2014.

9. Anon. (2014). *Author information in search results.* Available: https://support.google.com/webmasters/answer/1408986. Last accessed 26 June 2014.

10. Anon. (2014). *Data limits.* Available: https://support.google.com/analytics/answer/1070983?hl=en-GB. Last accessed Aug 2014.

11. Anon. (2014). *Do you need an SEO?* Available: https://support.google.com/webmasters/answer/35291?hl=en. Last accessed May 2014.

12. Anon. (2014). *Domain.* Available: http://moz.com/learn/seo/domain. Last accessed Aug 2014.

13. Anon. (2014). *Google Algorithm Change History.* Available: http://moz.com/google-algorithm-change. Last accessed Aug 2014.

14. Anon. (2014). *Google Annual Search Statistics.* Available: http://www.statisticbrain.com/google-searches/. Last accessed 19 Aug 2014.

15. Anon. (2014). *Introduction to Google Analytics.* Available: https://support.google.com/analytics/answer/1008065?hl=en-GB. Last accessed May 2014.

16. Anon. (2014). *Use canonical URLs.* Available:

https://support.google.com/webmasters/answer/13 9066?hl=en. Last accessed July 2014.

17.   Anon. (unknown). *Categories for Types of Websites.* Available: http://orthodoxdaily.com/types-of-websites/. Last accessed July 2014.

18.   Anon. (unknown). *Google Indexed Page Checker.* Available: http://www.northcutt.com/tools/free-seo-tools/google-indexed-pages-checker/. Last accessed Aug 2014.

19.   Anon. (unknown). *PageSpeed Insights.* Available: https://developers.google.com/speed/pagespeed/in sights/. Last accessed Aug 2014.

20.   Anon. (unknown). *The Beginners Guide to SEO.* Available: http://static.seomoz.org/files/SEOmoz-The-Beginners-Guide-To-SEO-2012.pdf. Last accessed May 2014.

21.   Capper, T. (2014). *Setting Up 4 Key Customer Loyalty Metrics in Google Analytics.* Available: http://moz.com/blog/customer-loyalty-metrics-google-analytics. Last accessed July 1st 2014.

22.   Carswell, J. (2014). *A Change to Close Variant Keyword Matching in AdWords.* Available: http://www.periscopix.co.uk/blog/a-change-to-close-variant-keyword-matching-in-adwords/?utm_source=LinkedIn&utm_medium=So cial&utm_campaign=Blog. Last accessed Aug 2014.

23.   Fishkin, R. (2011). *Google's Farmer/Panda Update: Analysis of Winners vs. Losers.* Available: http://moz.com/blog/googles-farmer-update-

analysis-of-winners-vs-losers. Last accessed Jan 2014.

24.   Goodwin, D. (2011). *Google Losing War With Scraper Sites Asks For Help.* Available: http://searchenginewatch.com/article/2105023/Google-Losing-War-With-Scraper-Sites-Asks-For-Help. Last accessed Mar 2014.

25.   Levy, S. (2011). *TED 2011: The 'Panda' That Hates Farms: A Q&A with Google's Top Search Engineers.* Available: http://www.wired.com/2011/03/the-panda-that-hates-farms. Last accessed Feb 2014.

26.   Lyons, K. (2013). *Boost your blog's SEO mojo, with these 6 simple actionable steps.* . Available: http://searchenginewatch.com/article/2270685/Boost-Your-Blogs-SEO-Mojo-with-These-6-Simple-Actionable-Steps. Last accessed May 2014.

27.   McCullagh, D. (2011). *Testing Google's Panda algorithm: CNET analysis.* Available: http://www.cnet.com/news/testing-googles-panda-algorithm-cnet-analysis/. Last accessed Feb 2014.

28.   McGee, M. (2014). *Google's Pigeon Update Solves Yelp Problem, Boosts Local Directories.* Available: http://searchengineland.com/googles-pigeon-update-solves-yelp-problem-boosts-local-directories-197949. Last accessed July 2014.

29.   Meyers, P. (2014). *The Month Google Shook the SERPs.* Available: http://moz.com/blog/the-month-google-shook-the-serps. Last accessed Aug 2014.

30.   Mueller, John. (2014). *Author information in search results.* Available:

https://plus.google.com/+JohnMueller/posts. Last accessed 26 June 2014.

31.   Ntoulas, A. (2006). *Detecting Spam Web Pages through Content Analysis.* Available: http://research.microsoft.com/pubs/65140/www200 6.pdf. Last accessed December 2013.

32.   Redsicker, P. (2014). *18 Social Media SEO Resources to Improve Your Search Ranking.* Available: http://www.socialmediaexaminer.com/social-media-seo/. Last accessed Mar 2014.

33.   Roach, K. (2012). *600+ Places to Share Your Content and Get MORE Traffic....* Available: http://www.buzzblogger.com/600-places-to-share-your-content/. Last accessed Mar 2014.

34.   Schwartz, B. (2014). *Google "Pigeon" Updates Local Search Algorithm with Stronger Ties to Web Search Signal.* Available: http://searchengineland.com/google-makes-significant-changes-local-search-ranking-algorithm-197778. Last accessed July 2014.

35.   Segal, D.. (2011). *The Dirty Little Secrets of Search.* Available: http://www.nytimes.com/2011/02/13/business/13se arch.html?pagewanted=all&_r=1&. Last accessed Jan 2014.

36.   Smarty, A. (2008). *Ann Smarty December 17, 2008 24SHARES11COMMENTS 22 2 SEOrefugee thread opened up a great discussion on what BlackHat SEO literally is. I also got definitions from Google and Wikipedia in an effort t.* Available: http://www.searchenginejournal.com/what-is-blackhat-seo-5-definitions/8151/. Last accessed December 2013.

37.   Sullivan, D.. (2014). *Leaked Documents Show How Yelp Thinks It's Not Getting Screwed By Google.* Available: http://searchengineland.com/leaked-documents-yelp-google-196208. Last accessed July 2014.

38.   Sullivan, D.. (October 2008). *What Is Search Engine Spam? The Video Edition.* Available: http://searchengineland.com/what-is-search-engine-spam-the-video-edition-15202. Last accessed December 2013.

39.   Seiter, C. (2014). *The Complete Beginner's Guide to SEO.* Available: http://www.huffingtonpost.com/courtney-seiter/the-complete-beginners-gu_b_5454161.html . Last accessed June 2014.

40.   Dean, B. (2013). *[Infographic] Google's 200 Ranking Factors.* Available: http://www.searchenginejournal.com/infographic-googles-200-ranking-factors/64316/. Last accessed Jan 2014.

41.   Anon. (unknown). *unknown.* Available: https://www.google.com/intl/en/insidesearch/howsearchworks/thestory/ . Last accessed Aug 2014.

42.   Anon. (unknown). *The Knowledge Graph.* Available: http://www.google.com/insidesearch/features/search/knowledge.html. Last accessed Aug 2014.